MONOLITHIC ARCHITECTURE

Rodolfo Machado
Rodolphe el-Khoury

The Heinz Architectural Center,
The Carnegie Museum of Art, Pittsburgh

MONOLITHIC ARCHITECTURE

Rodolfo Machado and
Rodolphe el-Khoury

With Essays by
Detlef Mertins
Spiro N. Pollalis
Paulette Singley
and Wilfried Wang

The Heinz Architectural Center
The Carnegie Museum of Art,
Pittsburgh

Prestel
Munich · New York

This catalogue has been published in conjunction
with the exhibition **Monolithic Architecture**,
held at The Heinz Architectural Center,
The Carnegie Museum of Art, Pittsburgh,
30 September 1995–11 February 1996.

Editors Rodolfo Machado and Rodolphe el-Khoury
Assistant Editor Mark Pasnik
Manuscript Editor Andrea P.A. Belloli, London

Cover Jean Nouvel, The New National Theater,
Tokyo, Japan. North elevation
Frontispiece Philipe Starck, The Baron Vert

Die Deutsche Bibliothek–CIP Einheitsaufnahme:
Monolithic Architecture / [first published in the occasion of the
exhibition "Monolithic Architecture", helt at The Heinz
Architectural Center, The Carnegie Museum of Art, Pittsburgh,
30 September 1995–11 February 1996] Rodolfo Machado and
Rodolphe el-Khoury. With essays by Detlef Mertins. ... – Munich ;
New York : Prestel 1995
ISBN 3-7913-1609-5
NE: Machado, Rodolpho; Exhibition Monolithic Architecture.
»1995-1996 Pittsburgh, Pa .«; Heinz Architectural Center
»Pittsburgh, Pa.«

Prestel-Verlag
Mandlstrasse 26, 80802 Munich, Germany
Phone 4989 381 7090, Fax 4989 381 70935
and 16 West 22nd Street
New York, NY 10010, USA
Phone 212 627 8199, Fax 212 627 9866

Cover Design: Rainer Lienemann, Munich
Typeset by: Sheila de Vallée,
GB-Windsor Forest SL4 2EH
Offset lithography by i.b. Repro GmbH, Munich
Printed by Pera Druck Matthias GmbH, Gräfelfing
Bound by R. Oldenbourg, Munich
Printed in Germany
ISBN 3-7913-1609-5

THE ESSAYS

THE PROJECTS

Descriptions written by Mark Pasnik
(From statements provided by the architects)

The Carnegie Museum of Art is one of the few American museums with a full curatorial department devoted to architecture. This department was launched in 1990 through a founding gift of the Drue Heinz Trust made to honor Henry J. Heinz II. The Heinz Architectural Center opened to the public in the fall of 1993. From space originally designed by Alden and Harlow in 1907 and redesigned in 1974 by Edward Larabee Barnes, architects Pietro Cicognani and Ann Kalla created four changing exhibition galleries, a study room, collection storage, and curatorial offices. In addition, they incorporated Frank Lloyd Wright's San Francisco field office from the 1950s as a permanent exhibition.

Since opening, the Center has demonstrated its commitment to a range of interests. Curator Christopher Monkhouse is developing a collection of distinction, one emphasis of which is the representation of professional architectural delineators, another of which is institutional architecture related to the diversity of Carnegie Institute and its sister institution, Carnegie Library of Pittsburgh — namely museum and library buildings. The collection's formal and stylistic interests are rooted in the history of Pittsburgh and radiate from there both historically, whether to source or to influence, and geographically, both nationally and internationally.

The Center's exhibitions have begun to chart its intended course. Architecture of the region was the focus of *Pittsburgh Architecture, c. 1990*. Architects whose contributions have significantly altered the history of building were the subject of *Architecture in a Well Ordered Universe: Lord Burlington's Villa at Chiswick* and *Thomas Jefferson's Grounds for the University of Virginia* (organized respectively with the Canadian Centre for Architecture, Montreal, and the Royal Academy of Arts, London; and by the Bayly Art Museum of the University of Virginia) and *Karl Friedrich Schinkel, 1781–1841: The Drama of Architecture* (organized by the Art Institute of Chicago). While early in 1994, the Museum hosted the traveling exhibition *Renzo Piano Building Workshop, Monolithic Architecture* is the Center's first original contribution to the understanding of contemporary architecture in an international context. As Christopher Monkhouse makes clear in his preface, it is not coincidental that this exhibition is appearing at the Museum simultaneously with the 1995 Carnegie International.

On behalf of the Board of Trustees and staff of The Carnegie Museum of Art, I wish to acknowledge Mr. Monkhouse and his colleagues, Dennis McFadden and Rebecca Sciullo, the team that launched this project, and to extend heartfelt thanks to the curators who conceived and developed the exhibition, Rodolfo Machado and Rodolphe el-Khoury. I also want to mention the many contributions made by their dedicated and resourceful assistant editor, Mark Pasnik, and by

Anita Breslaw and the staff of the Department of Urban Planning and Design, Graduate School of Design, Harvard University. To the architects who have participated and the authors who have contributed essays to the catalogue, I also express our profound gratitude. We have thoroughly enjoyed our collaboration with Prestel-Verlag in the creation of this publication and credit Andrea P.A. Belloli, in particular, for its accomplishment. I would also like to acknowledge the Centre National d'Art et de Culture Georges Pompidou, Paris, and Meisei Engineering Company, Ltd., for their generous loans to the exhibition. Finally, to Drue Heinz and the Drue Heinz Trust we are indebted both for the creation of The Heinz Architectural Center, which has given the Museum an extraordinary opportunity in the field of architecture, and for support of *Monolithic Architecture*.

Phillip M. Johnston
The Henry J. Heinz II Director
The Carnegie Museum of Art

Preface

Had Andrew Carnegie been alive for the centennial of the institution he opened in 1895, he would probably have been pleased to encounter *Monolithic Architecture* in the exhibition galleries of The Heinz Architectural Center. Global in its point of view, and with all projects conceived during the last decade, *Monolithic Architecture* is much in keeping with Carnegie's philosophy to exhibit the international old masters of the future.

Almost as soon as Carnegie Institute opened its doors in Pittsburgh, the local chapter of the American Institute of Architects and its closely related Pittsburgh Architectural Club were being encouraged to hold meetings there, as well as exhibitions of contemporary architecture. Initiated in 1898, the exhibition program first achieved true international significance with the fourth exhibition assembled by the Pittsburgh Architectural Club at the Institute in 1907.

On view for the month of November 1907 and housed in the recently opened galleries provided by a second donation of bricks and mortar by Andrew Carnegie which more than doubled the size of the original building, the fourth exhibition consisted of more than 1,500 exhibits, making it the largest architectural show organized in America up to that time. In addition to its size, the fourth exhibition enjoyed a number of firsts, including 12 works by Frank Lloyd Wright, who up to that point had not exhibited his work publicly outside the Chicago area. The gallery devoted to modern European work gave many Americans their first opportunity to compare current practice abroad with that in their own country. Outstanding examples of modern design from the British Isles were provided by Charles Rennie Mackintosh, Margaret Macdonald Mackintosh, and Halsey Ricardo, while the work of H. P. Berlage and Carl Moser, among others, spoke for the Continent. That the significance of this event did not go unheralded can be seen from the broad coverage it received in the professional press, not to mention the attendance figures, which reached 88,000 visitors before the exhibition closed.

Pittsburgh did not have another opportunity to host such a broad survey of modern architecture until The Carnegie Museum took the traveling version of the Museum of Modern Art's *Modern Architecture — International Exhibition* in 1933. In order to make sure that the significance of that exhibition was not overlooked, local architect Robert Schmertz provided an insightful review of it in *Carnegie Magazine*. More than 60 years intervened until the Museum again focused on current architectural trends both here and abroad. This renewed interest in recent architecture was made possible through the opening of The Heinz Architectural Center in 1993.

The 1995 centennial of The Carnegie Museum of Art's global survey of contemporary art, known as the Carnegie International, presented The Heinz Architectural Center with a special opportunity to organize a complementary review of recent architecture. In so doing, it recalled that the other major survey of modern art begun in the 1890s, the Venice Biennale, introduced architecture into its 39th edition in 1980. Organized by Paolo Portoghesi, with a committee including Robert Stern and Vincent Scully, the inaugural event for architecture in the context of the Biennale was made memorable by the Strada Novissima housed in the old ropeworks of the Arsenal. One of the architects who participated was Rodolfo Machado. Argentinean by birth, Mr. Machado had an architectural practice in Pittsburgh in the mid-1970s while teaching at Carnegie Mellon University. He is currently a principal in the Boston firm of Machado and Silvetti Associates and professor in practice of architecture and urban design in the Graduate School of Design at Harvard University. Following his participation in the Venice Biennale in 1980, he made contributions to the third and fifth Biennales for Architecture in 1985 and 1991, making him particularly well qualified to serve as co-curator of an exhibition of contemporary architecture intended to coincide with the Carnegie International during its centennial.

Mr. Machado in turn invited Rodolphe el-Khoury to co-curate *Monolithic Architecture*. Born in Lebanon, Mr. el-Khoury is assistant professor of urban planning and design in the Graduate School of Design, Harvard University, and a partner in the Boston firm of Office dA. His broad view of current trends complements that of Mr. Machado. Together they defined the theme of the exhibition, identified the projects to illustrate this theme, and selected authors to comment on the place of monolithic architecture in current practice and theoretical debate in this catalogue. Thus representing 14 countries, *Monolithic Architecture* provides an excellent geographic fit with the 1995 Carnegie International. And as monolithic architecture is inherently sculptural, there should be a number of provocative formal parallels with the works of art shown in the adjacent galleries as part of the International, making architecture's presence in this centennial year all the more poignant.

Christopher Monkhouse
Curator
The Heinz Architectural Center

Rodolfo Machado
Rodolphe el-Khoury

Monolithic Architecture

Once when I was six years old I saw a magnificent picture in a book, called <u>True Stories from Nature</u>, about the primeval forest. It was a picture of a boa constrictor in the act of swallowing an animal. Here is a copy of the drawing. In the book it said: „Boa constrictors swallow their prey whole, without chewing it. After that they are not able to move, and they sleep through the six months that they need for digestion."

I pondered deeply, then, over the adventures of the jungle. And after some work with a colored pencil I succeeded in making my first drawing. My Drawing Number One. It looked like this:

I showed my masterpiece to the grown-ups, and asked them whether the drawing frightened them. But they answered: "Frighten? Why should any one be frightened by a hat?"

My drawing was not a picture of a hat. It was a picture of a boa constrictor digesting an elephant. But since the grown-ups were not able to understand it, I made another drawing: I drew the inside of the boa constrictor, so that the grown-ups could see it clearly. They always need to have things explained. My Drawing Number Two looked like this:

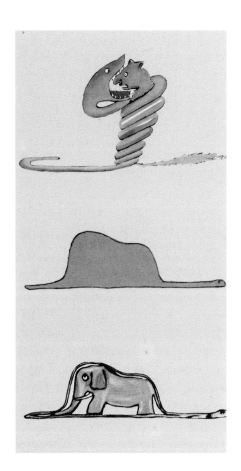

A number of recent architectural works have converged on features and issues that, in our view, merit investigation. Some of these works have already acquired notoriety, due primarily to their strong physical presence in important urban settings. Most are still under construction or were never actually implemented in built form. Nevertheless, they circulate in drawings and model reproductions, yielding sporadic jolts of critical controversy with occasional appearances in various architectural journals. These buildings, at first glance, seem to have little in common; in fact, their blatant differences in shape, material, scale, and program could hardly warrant an exhibition claiming aesthetic coherence. Indeed, any attempt to identify common formal or stylistic traits across the emphatic individuality of these buildings is at best a contrived artifice and, more probably, a coercive imposition of conformity upon highly individuated expressions.

Yet, these buildings coincide in their extreme economy and simplicity of overall form and consistency of external appearance; also common is their capacity to deliver tremendous eloquence with very limited formal means. Some adopt straightforward, elementary configurations, while others limit more gestural impulses to a clear and single utterance. Sometimes, they construct their clarity with one or two bold spaces; more characteristically, they contain considerable planimetric and sectional complexities within strict volumetric restraint. All have a monolithic character that ostensibly defies current preoccupations with arbitrariness, shapelessness, fragmentation, and heterogeneity.

Such emphatic simplicity and consistency in the composition of the exterior evokes various episodes in the history of architecture. Yet, a consistent unorthodoxy in the treatment of building types, programs, materials, and technologies marks important distinctions and denies any particular or clear pedigree. It may be tempting to seek distant relatives to monolithic architecture among some (neo)classical, modernist, and (neo)rationalist architectures or even in non-Western building practices. But besides a common investment in the power of primary forms, obvious formal and ideological differences within monolithic architecture and with respect to such precedents problematize linear genealogies. For instance, this architecture does not articulate the part in relation to the whole as dictated by classical doctrine, nor does it avoid inconsistencies between exterior and interior character and disposition. Quite the contrary, most of the buildings gathered in this volume insist on such disjunctions, and, unlike much twentieth-century architecture, they are not compelled to externalize the complexity of the program in individuated iconographic or volumetric components, nor do they shy away from a mannerist confusion of structure and ornament. More critical is the distinction between the taciturn elementarism of modernism and the *monodic poetry* of the architectural monolith, between negational silence and *rhetorical laconism*. The simplicity of the architectural monolith does not aim at abstraction, nor does it share the minimalist aspiration to nonreferential objecthood. Rather, it seeks to maximize the expressive potential of common architectonic configurations by condensing their figurative allusions into one eloquent gesture.

In short, a disdain for stylistic rigor, historical veracity, structural rectitude, or other claims at transcendence and authenticity clearly positions this architecture in the contemporary cultural arena, among other postmodern contestants that have embraced the schizophrenic tensions of culture and society. Monolithic architecture thrives in the unprecedented conditions of today's megalopolis. Its strategic schematism is calibrated to the specific urban and suburban conditions of late capitalist environments. It is sometimes tailored to the company of dignified buildings in so-called historical districts, places whose aura has the unfortunate tendency to inspire degrading spectacles of simulated authenticity from traditionalists and avant-gardists alike. However, the radical composure of monolithic architecture is most often customized for the challenging environments of consumerism. With its assumed gravity, it is meant to sober the strident gesticulations of neighboring buildings in congested city centers and to generate with its stubborn presence a sense of urbanity in more depleted surroundings.

Questions concerning success or failure at these ambitious tasks will be left aside for the moment, since there is no objective way to verify or falsify claims about the instrumentality of monolithic character in the construction of urbanity. In the context of this discussion, problems of representation are also of greater relevance than issues of construction and usage per se. We prefer to focus on tectonics rather than technology, and we will consider the program in its capacity to generate form and not in terms of functional efficiency. We wish to examine these buildings in their most radical aspect, as *paradoxical representations*: radical, in the sense that they self-consciously elaborate their monolithic character into an aesthetic strategy and carry it out to its extreme realization; paradoxical, in the sense that they undermine their own fixity and solidity when their lapidary countenance stands as something totally other with respect to internal and external realities, program, and context.

The stark muteness of the architectural monolith may have an alienating aspect; its hermetic consistency does not readily inspire sympathy nor facilitate empathy. But unlike the dumb boxes of commercial architecture — as epitomized by the American shopping mall — whose characteristic blankness is due to neglect, insensitivity, and financial economy, architectural monoliths are more egocentric than introverted, arrogant rather than aloof. Their external economy is achieved at the cost of formal and material excesses and calibrated for intended effects. We were struck by their sudden and ponderous apparition among the volatile fragments of the collaged landscape, intrigued by their unexpected and sometimes scandalous pedigree (who would have expected Peter Eisenman to father such a fascinating "monster" as the Max Reinhardt Haus?). We have acquired a taste for their uncanny beauty and have also come to recognize their critical potential in reasserting the object in current architectural production at the moment of its proclaimed dispersal and evaporation in multicultural societies, digital technologies, and virtual realities.

We like to consider the insistent and unapologetic "object-ness" of these buildings as a challenge to some conceptual habits and compositional clichés in the aesthetics of today's institutional avant-garde. The monolithic architectures examined in this volume and corollary exhibition blatantly transgress some of the formal principles now automatically associated with critical, emancipatory, or progressive architectural practices without having to retreat to conservative ideological positions or having to indulge a nostalgia for solidity, stability, and organic unity in relation to context. Simultaneously solid and hollow, uniform and heterogeneous, impregnable and permeable, foreign and familiar, *the monolith that is not one* stands out as a glitch, a disturbance within the dialectical logic and the corollary axiological dichotomies that continue to regulate the theoretical discourse in architecture and persistently sanction the emancipatory virtues of the formless as opposed to the totalizing and repressive authority of the "formed," the small to the big, the fragmented to the coherent, the transparent to the opaque, the irregular to the orthogonal.

We have gathered here a variety of buildings and projects under the banner of "monolithic architecture" in order to demonstrate different instances of its paradoxical representations. We do not intend to prescribe a coherent aesthetic from an exemplary body of work; we have faith, rather, in the diversity within the collection to keep stylistic claims and totalizing "isms" at bay — we are now all too aware of the marketing logic underlying the packaging of recent "isms" to indulge the complacency of their institutional legitimation. Desire, personal predilections, biases in taste no doubt have inflected the choice of examples and color this volume with a particular sensibility — a certain "style," one might argue. However, the investment — and the fascination — lies in the aberrant status of the architectural monoliths themselves, their extraordinary appearance in contemporary practice and within the oeuvre of particular architects. We present them as a set of isolated, but parallel anomalies rather than as the converging symptoms of a new tendency.

In the recent past, a number of exhibitions and publications have proposed various formal systems in an attempt to deal with the changing conditions of culture and society on the level of architectural representation. Such proposals have ranged from prescriptive demonstrations of compositional strategies and zeitgeist-invoking arguments about new styles and new spirits to theoretical critiques of representational codes and conventions. Operating with the persistent assumption that an authentic work reflects a real condition (material, cultural, or social) that is otherwise shrouded in ideology and inaccessible to consciousness (without the mediation of art), these proposals have promoted various architectonic systems by virtue of their reflective perspicacity: certain forms, modes of construction, or tectonics are better suited than others because their specular power can pierce through ideological veils to get at the "real." The "real" may be an unalienated essence that is symbolized organically in a regionalist idiom or, more fashionably, a heterogeneous nexus of contradictions and discontinuities which is translated in the conflictual fragments of an architectural collage. Regardless of content, ideology, and politics, the theoretical legitimations of the various styles coincide in their insistence on overlapping architectonic configurations with structures and narratives in nature and culture.

We make no such claims for architectural monoliths. Rather, we tend to view them as opaque spots in the field of representation, opaque in the sense that they are not readily transparent to any particular homology with social formations or allegory of political engagement.

Latent Monoliths

The possibility of designing architectural monoliths exists in a mostly dormant condition. It appears that a monolith "is committed," like a sin, a bad action of sorts or a mean act committed by an *enfant terrible*.

In certain cases (Peter Eisenman, for instance), the monolithic moment appears as a lapse in ongoing research on the production of architectural form or as the manifestation of a repressed desire through the mediation of automated design. In other cases (Rem Koolhaas, most clearly), the monolith appears almost as a reversal of the habitual mode of work, as a "let's try it" moment from which results, in this particular example, a seemingly "corseted body" (its laces becoming roads connecting it to the city lying at its waist) replete with programs, typologies, and formal configurations of many kinds. For Rafael Moneo, whose architecture is, at the formal level, particularly varied, his monoliths appear as a didactic instance, the teaching of a lesson, the setting of an example. (This reading is possible after studying his entire oeuvre, in which his architecture consistently displays an exemplary quality). With Jean Nouvel and Farshid Moussavi/Alejandro Zaera-Polo, the monolith may be seen as a radicalization of latent tendencies, while for Philippe Starck (the monolith-maker par excellence) it appears as the obsessive reiteration of the same idea. In the partnerships of Jacques Herzog and Pierre de Meuron and Simon Ungers and Tom Kinslow, the monolith represents a refinement of evolving research into essentialism and reductivism.

Composite Monoliths

Unlike the archaic monolith, which is ideally carved out of a single block (fig. 1), monolithic architecture is assembled from parts. The only modern architecture that is truly monolithic is that of the bunker (fig. 2). As an extreme instance of monolithic architecture, the bunker could be held to radicalize some characteristic properties of monolithic architecture. One architectural theorist has suggested that the bunker manifests the repressed tendencies of architecture in general: its unavowed complicity with the war machine. We need not follow the theoretical intricacies of this radical claim to notice features of the bunker in some architectural monoliths: the tilting volumes of Moneo's Kursaal Cultural Center and Auditorium bear an uncanny resemblance to the toppled casemates of the Normandy beaches; the windows of Starck's Baron Vert recall the loopholes of fortified observation towers; the siting, character, and demeanor of Ungers and Kinslow's T-House are vaguely bunkerlike.

Fig. 1. View of the unfinished obelisk which remains in its pharaonic quarry near Assuan, Egypt.

These resemblances are nevertheless purely physiognomic, however, since the buildings we are dealing with here do not even approximate the thorough homogeneity and solidity of bunkers. Not only are they assembled from discrete building elements, but they sometimes contain contrasting programmatic units that are distinguished by different geometries, structural systems, and materials. This disparity is only reconciled on the surface, in a unified and continuous envelope that only occasionally yields glimpses into the spatial complexity of the interior. A subtle flutter, a minute disturbance in the pattern of the cladding, a barely perceptible deformation of the geometry suffice to suggest an inner turmoil that is never allowed to disrupt the architecture's costumed composure.

Great ingenuity is often required in fitting complex programs within the strict frame of the monolith's tailored simplicity. In a tour de force of volumetric composition, some contrive elaborate sequences of highly differentiated spaces within a pristine and regular container. Others achieve the "monolith effect" by dedicating the greatest visible portion of the building to a single important component of the program, while arranging auxiliary functions into backdrop slabs, unobtrusive plinths, or concealed basement levels (Dominique Perrault's project for the Bibliothèque de France comes to mind [fig. 3]). Dexterity in the manipulation of the program is required in both cases: it does not aim to streamline the function of the building (some monoliths have actually created controversy with supposedly ill-functioning plans); rather, the programmatic ingenuity seeks rhetorical clarity in the articulation of the overall figure and the uncompromising continuity and consistency of its surface.

Fig. 2. Paul Virilio, World War II observation post on the Normandy coast. Reproduced from Paul Virilio, Bunker archéologie (Paris: Centre Georges Pompidou, 1975), p. 103.

Hollow Monoliths

With the exception of monuments, architecture requires spaces for inhabitation. If the term *monolithic* is taken literally to suggest material solidity, monolithic architecture would be impossible by definition. However intrigued we might be by the oxymoron, we understand *monolithic* to signify *monolith-like*, and hence to confer a sense of solidity and homogeneity on objects that are not and could not be integrally solid and homogeneous. Still, the necessary hollowness of most buildings is such that the use of the term *monolithic* usually operates *metaphorically*, as a hyperbolic indication of exceptional uniformity and integrity in a given structure. We would also like to suggest an *allegorical* usage of *monolithic* for buildings that do not have the physical and material properties of the monolith, but that seem, "pretend," or "act" as though they do. In its allegorical mode, the term *monolithic* has more to do with *representational strategies* than material qualities. In the context of this exhibition, the monolith is primarily a representational model; there is, however, a potential for more literal or material adaptations of the monolith as a constructional model, as is suggested by the T-House and Yokohama International Port Terminal. This potential has yet to be fully explored with the ingenious use of new materials and building technologies.

Sponge or Swiss-cheese-like structures might offer an opportunity for *literally* monolithic architecture, because they are hollow *and* solid, voids being integral to their formal and material structure. Paradoxically, such configurations would allow for inhabitation within "solid" mass, in the structural cavities of the material, but would pose obvious challenges (technological and programmatic) for their architectural implementation. One of the closest realizations of this model is Koolhaas's proposal for the Bibliothèque de France (fig. 4). This project — which will remain unbuilt, perhaps because of its bewildering radicality — synthesizes conventional modes of construction and occupancy with a Swiss-cheese-type spatial model. The resulting building is unmistakably monolithic, despite occasional transparencies and internal inconsistencies: a laminated cubic block, filled with book stacks, in which public spaces are carved out or trapped like air pockets and fossils in crystalline resin.

Unless they have programs involving voluminous mechanical equipment — such as power plants — or extended storage space — such as libraries — few architectural monoliths display the rather quixotic pursuit of thorough and literal solidity. They demonstrate, instead, an exacerbated disparity between solid surface and hollow body. The disparity is thematic: the tensions between the literal and the phenomenal, the interior and the exterior, the physiognomical and anatomical are systematically exploited as catalysts for architectural invention, erecting the *hollow solidity* of architectural monoliths into paradoxical representations.

Fig. 3. Dominique Perrault, Bibliothèque Nationale de France, 1989: model. Reproduced from Dominique Perrault, <u>Dominique Perrault</u> (Zurich: Artemis, 1994), p. 52.

Epidermal Monoliths

In much of monolithic architecture, the representational elaboration of the "monolithic" is carried out along and across the limit between the interior and the exterior. "Monolithic architecture," we may say, is concentrated *in the thickness of the envelope, in the surface.* The skin-deep monolith is nevertheless to be distinguished from semiological conceptions of architecture, such as Robert Venturi's "decorated shed," primarily in its tendency to erase altogether the distinction between "decoration" and "shed," but also in the monosyllabic character of its "message." It lacks the syntactic articulation of traditional architectural languages and is often reduced to a single utterance that has the energy and universal resonance of an interjection.

The surface of the monolith is furthermore treated as an autonomous system. Unlike the traditional building facade or elevation, whose formal and material qualities are negotiated between internal conditions (programmatic, planimetric, sectional) and external contextual pressures, the surface of the monolith is characteristically independent of such constraints: it is designed with distinct and often uncompromising formal features that tend to set it apart from the "body" of the building. This "detachment" is rendered spatial in a more or less literal fashion and confers a shell-like quality to the skin. The shell could still have physiognomic features, but they are abstracted or stylized. If the traditional elevation is understood as the epidermal registration of the genetic and somatic qualities of an architectural body, then the surface of the monolith should evoke the armor, the cuirass, and the helmet: inorganic and redundant skins with simulated bodily and facial features.

As an autonomous architectural system, the surface encapsulates (contains) the building in more than one sense: it is deployed three-dimensionally so as to wrap more or less complex programs into one package, much like the fabric of an installation by Christo and Jeanne-Claude (fig. 5). Within its limited thickness and with its volumetric expression, it is also meant to condense and deliver the architectural effect that would customarily build up evenly and consistently throughout the building. Think of how much architecture is packed, within a few millimeters of thickness, into the curtain walls of Nouvel's or Moneo's architecture.

This surface may be hard, polished, and highly reflective. It may have a discernible thickness in the texture of the revetment and even greater physical depth in the layering of more or less transparent cladding membranes. But the ambition is the same: to endow surface with depth, literal or phenomenal. In some instances, the experience of depth is primarily visual, as in Nouvel's New National Theater, where polished stone cladding reflects the surrounding city and the sky above, occasionally yielding glimpses of the interior through glass panels flush-mounted against granite slabs. Philippe Samyn's Walloon Forestry Department Shell invites a more tactile gaze to fondle its intricately layered surface, to probe into faintly discernible depths. In Moneo's Kursaal, the cladding system of the outer shell is literally deep and could accommodate tactile apprehension and potentially allow for bodily inhabitation. The depth of the surface is most substantial in the Yokohama International Port Terminal: the whole building is collapsed into the surface, whose topological articulations define spaces for programmatic differentiation and human occupancy.

In addition to formal autonomy, the envelope of the monolith can also have inherent rigidity and structural support. The formal and structural autonomy of the envelope was taken to such an extreme in the Tokyo New National Theater that Nouvel had to multiply the analogies in order to convey the extent to which it deviated from traditional architectural solutions. He describes the building as a crucible, a case for musical instruments, a coffer, a box, rather than in the traditional architectural terminology of walls, elevations, and facades. These analogies are meant to be taken as literally as possible. Nouvel is not speaking here of box-like architecture, but — more radically — of an architectural box or of *architecture-as-box*. In his own words, architecture as *capotage*, or "hooding."

Monolithic architecture overlaps here with industrial design in the tendency to treat the building as an object, like an appliance or a vehicle. The envelope — we may also call it an encasement, cover, or hood — is designed as a separate problem with the intent to contain the internal complexity within a compact and hermetic package that has a recognizable and distinct form. New formal categories and taxonomies are needed for describing this architectural encasement, and clues are available in design products.

The typologies of musical instrument cases (fig. 6) offer, for instance, three broad categories that might prove useful in identifying different types of mono-

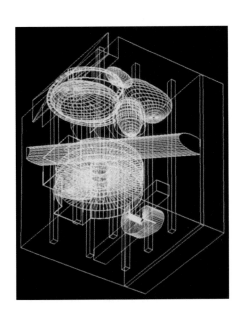

Fig. 4. Rem Koolhaas, Bibliothèque Nationale de France, 1989: computer-generated axonometric drawing. Courtesy Office for Metropolitan Architecture.

lithic architectures. One common type of case — we shall call it type A — has a rectangular or trapezoidal shape and includes a poché layer of soft material to mediate between its generic geometry and the particular contours of the instruments inside. Koolhaas's Sea Terminal, Samyn's Walloon Forestry Department Shell and Moneo's Kursaal would fall into this first category. They all contrast regularized external volumes with eccentric interior structures whose particular forms are tailored to specific programs. Another type of case — type B — betrays faintly the contours of the instrument while negotiating the regularity of its geometry with subtle curves, depressions, and protuberances. This is precisely how the distortions of the black granite shell register the three theaters inside Nouvel's New National Theatre. The third type of case — type C — espouses more or less faithfully the shape of the contained object in a moldlike fashion and secures it tightly in place while providing added protection. In Ungers and Kinslow's T-House, the boxes of finished living spaces are accordingly encased in monolithic oxidized steel shells, while the concrete structure of Herzog and de Meuron's Signal Box auf dem Wolf is lodged in a coil of copper ribbons

It may be tempting here to revisit Venturi's categories of "duck" and "shed" if only to demonstrate their inadequacy in this particular context. In the typology just constructed, the autonomy of the outer envelope amounts to a kind of structural doubling in the architecture: the building wraps itself with a building. This *mise-en-abîme* explodes Venturi's dyadic structure into a complex matrix and allows for unexpected permutations that eventually undermine the framework altogether: a type-A monolith might qualify as a shed — or is it a duck? — but what about types B and C, where duck and shed seem to be ambiguously superimposed? Or should one distinguish between outer shed and internal duck, or vice versa? Is Nouvel's New National Theater a duck or a shed? A duck that has swallowed three sheds? Or, in Starck's own words, a "whale that has swallowed the Kaa'ba?" According to Venturi's definition, it may simply be described as a duck, a building "where the architectural systems of space, structure, and program are submerged and distorted by an overall symbolic form," but paradoxically, this duck is in the form of a shed.

Fig. 5. Christo and Jeanne-Claude, <u>Wrapped Reichstag</u>, 1971-1995, copyright Christo, 1995. Photo: Jürgen Gebhardt/Peter Thomann. Reproduced from <u>Stern</u>, 29 June 1995, p. 20.

Floating Monoliths

Universality is a common trait of architectural monoliths. The simplicity and integrity of their geometry does not easily accommodate contextual inflections. In fact, their self-possessed posture seems to arrogantly dismiss such external influences. Monolithic architecture is in this sense antithetical to regionalism, be it critical or otherwise. Some isolated examples do adopt local material, modes of construction, or even indigenous types, yet their uncompromised formal integrity cannot but affirm their (in)difference. Much like the black parallelepiped which stood as the pure Other against the primordial landscape in *2001: A Space Odyssey*, monolithic architecture is a stranger in any context (fig. 7). So singular is its enigmatic detachment from its immediate surroundings that in time, the monolith invariably becomes an icon of the place. This metonymic shift can take hold instantly, as is demonstrated by the history of the Eiffel Tower's reception. That the alien building should represent, embody, or simply become the site that defines its alterity is a paradox that will unravel any narrow categorization of monolithic architecture with respect to site and context.

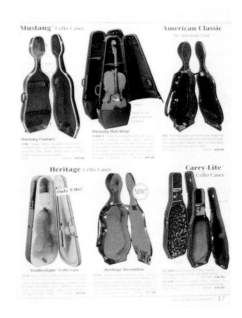

Fig. 6. Musical instrument cases. Reproduced from <u>Shar Products Company Catalogue</u>, Spring 1993, p. 17.

The ambivalent detachment of this architecture is occasionally articulated in the tectonics of the envelope. For instance, rootlessness is emphasized in the omission of a differentiated base and top or in the continuity of cladding patterns across horizontal and vertical surfaces — with total disregard for architectural conventions and the laws of statics. This uniform treatment of external surfaces is a recurrent device in monolithic architecture: it is meant to suggest homogeneous and autonomous object-ness. Architectural monoliths accordingly lack apparent foundations; they seem to be grounded merely by gravity, deposited on the ground by divine hands. Often, one finds them leaning sideways as if sinking slowly into the soil, because of their excessive weight, through years of imperceptible settlement.

The excessive weight is most often illusory. In fact, some architectural monoliths capitalize on sophisticated technology to convey impressions of the heaviest weight with the lightest of structures. With the notable exception of Samyn's Walloon Forestry Department Shell, none of the buildings under discussion here aim at a "transparent" expression of the structure's physical properties. New materials and technologies are used as a means for efficient support and rhetorical ends that may even pervert supposedly "natural" predispositions. Witness the "insane" superimposition of Möbius-strip geometry on a steel frame structure in Eisenman's Max Reinhardt Haus.

Even more paradoxical is the vehicular character of many architectural monoliths, their tendency to contradict the most static of dispositions with a figurative suggestion of mobility. Hence the predilection for balloons, dirigibles, spaceships, aircraft carriers, submarines, images of grounded vessels and frozen movement which convey a double longing for imminent departure and permanent rest, reiterating the buildings' ambivalence with regard to context. Nomadic tendencies and global allegiances are expressed most literally in the Green Building by Future Systems, an ovoid structure supported on leglike columns (fig. 8). The building complements its symbolic and formal detachment from context with an airtight, biosphere-like interior. Even the air one breathes inside this building is different.

Fig. 7. "The Dawn of Man." Still from Stanley Kubrick (director), <u>2001: A Space Odyssey</u> (1968). Reproduced from Stanley Kubrick (director), <u>2001: A Space Odyssey</u> (MGM/UA Home Video).

Digital Monoliths

It so happens that many of the monoliths we have examined have depended on various computer technologies for their elaboration. Computers were useful to some as drawing tools and essential to others in the construction phase: they served to control the machines that produce customized building components such as unusual metal extrusions or shaped synthetic surfaces. This is no mere coincidence: the relationship between computer-aided design (CAD) and monolithic architecture is not entirely circumstantial and could possibly account for the recent emergence of the latter — and, conversely, justify the utility of the former.

Computers abhor ornate forms and accidental volumes; they thrive instead on continuous surfaces with regular or gradually varying patterns — smooth, faceted, or folded. Surfaces with complex double curvatures, once a nightmare for draftsmen, framers, and stone cutters, are now commonplace features of the standard PC's 3-D modeling capabilities, while a "simple" Corinthian capital is difficult to plot on the most sophisticated of workstations.

Needless to say, the skin of the monolith, stretching across contorted volumes, conveniently smoothing over sectional irregularities with warping planes or triangulated facets, constitutes ideal CAD material. So obvious is the fit between object and tool that one is tempted to speak of a digital aesthetic, a formal vocabulary that is shaped by the expressive potential and limitations of this new mode of representation.

Monolithic architecture poses the following question: Has the digital paradigm unleashed a latent potential that was earlier contained by technical limits, or rather, has it created a new object, economically adapted to its representational means? Have the crude and stylized blocks of the still primitive models of virtual reality — shorthand notations of more complex referents — already transformed reality itself, in order to make it more readily simulatable?

Domesticated Monoliths

Like pets, these buildings receive affectionate names. Like places, they receive common names. Monolithic buildings are eminently nameable, and through the act of naming they become "ours." Simple, familiar nouns are easily cast at them by the public: thus, they become the iceberg, the wave, the rock, or the crystals; the box, the twins, the mound, or the totem; the ruffle, the curl, the lamp, or the tombstone; the balloon, the egg, the pebble, the whale, the Siamese twins, or the mount, etcetera, etcetera.

Additionally, they seem to induce viewers/speakers to shower them with adjectives and are prone to being the subject of rampant metaphors and associations:

— They look like gigantic Noguchi lamps!
— They appear to be wearing Issey Miyake pleats!
— Will they melt when summer comes?
— Will the skin rupture and the intestines drop into the sea?
— The ground has opened up, it's coming out!
— It's a dewdrop . . . or is it a pearl?
— They look like snakes . . .
— It's pregnant!
— Oh . . . look at it!
— Such flair, such style!
— It came from the moon, did it not?

In addition, it is evident that monolithic buildings possess a strange capacity for figuration, for adapting to the individual viewer's interpretive capacities (in a somewhat populist way, in a way in which traditional highbrow architecture does not), for being perhaps unforgettable. They are like an "accessory" pinned down to the urban fabric, like a brooch in a lapel. They are "props" on the urban stage (the necessary objects that allow the performance of an action that could not otherwise be enacted). They "decorate" the city, they "accent" it, they make it "it," they construct its identity. They are bragged about by the locals, they are proudly displayed, they belong to the city housing them.

They are loved, or they are hated. They do not inspire indifference.

Monolithic architecture always looks like something other than buildings. Such structures are eminently "morphic" (most commonly, they appear anthropomorphic or zoomorphic) or thinglike, rather than buildinglike. They become personable, and this condition provides one more means (or mode) of domestication. They are characters, actors, soloists; they have a persona, and this persona seems to emanate, tainting the nearby air in a selflike fashion. The air around them is colored: dark, ominous grays surround the T-House, aqueous blues are to be found above Moneo's project; acidic yellows hover over the Koolhaas design; electric greens and the Baron Vert are but one thing; tempestuous blacks surround the Signal Box; and so on.

Familiar Monoliths

Fig. 8. Future Systems, The Green Building, 1990: montage. Photo: Richard Davies. Reproduced from L'Arca, September 1991, p. 62.

For the culture of architecture and its audience, the formal languages at work in monolithic architecture — or, in other and more popular terms, its styling — appear to be disconcertingly familiar; in spite of the viewer's initial "shock" when first confronted with the monolithic, there seems to be an air of déjà vu about the languages employed in its materialization.

Thus, it is possible — and paradoxical, once again — to argue that these projects and buildings are somewhat revisionist, some of them even historicist. Most commonly, they seem to revisit, lovingly and at times critically, the architectures of the 1950s and 1960s, while the theoretical or marketing rhetoric that usually accompanies their promotion — by the client or the architect — insists on their novelty. It may be said that mid-twentieth-century modernity is monolithic architecture's preferred source material (just as neoclassical architecture was for postmodern architecture, historically considered).

Is the landscape on top of Farshid Moussavi and Alejandro Zaera-Polo's project not like the iconic landscape drawn by Superstudio in 1970 (fig. 9)? Are the people populating it, strangely inhabiting a topography of steel, not like the people in the endless abstracted ground of the Superstudio drawing? And are the interiors at times not like Eero Saarinen's interiors at the TWA Terminal? Valuable transformations have in fact occurred, but origins and references are clear and direct. Most appropriately, in the Max Reinhardt Haus one reads the expressionism of early twentieth-century German architecture, the mountaintops and crystals and crowns of Bruno Taut, but transformed, made of today. Given the design process established by Eisenman, it is unclear how much of this is intentional, how much is casual (it is perhaps a happy intersection of intentionalities). In the end, vis-à-vis the familiarity thus produced, it does not matter.

Looking further, can one see Moneo's project and not find refuge in Pierre Chareau to tame its monolithic nature? In Ungers and Kinslow, there are echoes of Mies, and there are echoes of Fuller (a pragmatic, nonutopian Fuller) in Samyn's work (the Mies in Ungers and Kinslow is visible close up, certainly not in the overall composition). Koolhaas effectively elaborates and reinterprets many 1960s moments, Brazilian moments (Oscar Niemeyer) and French ones, too (Jean Prouvé), certain science-fiction drawings, even certain fictional texts: there are moments in J.G. Ballard's *Crash* that conceivably could happen (or be staged in) the Koolhaas project.

Which brings us to that familiarity which is produced by reference not to architecture but to other practices, other products. The world of art (in this case, minimal art) informs Ungers and Kinslow, and abstract sculpture informs Nouvel. Obviously, industrial design (understood as a kind of art) pervades Starck's building, and in Herzog and de Meuron's work the exquisite world of the crafted object is there to illuminate it.

Penetrable Monoliths

The doorways of monolithic structures have historically posed challenging architectural problems. The history of the pyramid alone offers an extensive repertoire of frustrated entry designs, culminating in I.M. Pei's attempt at the Louvre. The difficulty is due to the resistence of the monolith to any kind of opening in its impervious surface, no matter how ingeniously it is designed. The resistence is partly justified in terms of formal consistency: the smooth and continuous planes of the monolith would be compromised by gaps, protruding frames, or appendages marking entrances. The breach in the surface is also an indication of hollowness, and this fact is far more threatening to the integrity of the monolith, which has to appear thoroughly solid for maximum effect. Even the most inconspicuous doorways and windows betray a hidden interiority, while the slightest fissure in the surface is tantamount to a gaping chasm. In the vulnerability of the orifice, solid mass irrevocably turns into cavernous void. Once penetrated, the obelisk becomes a cave.

Fig. 9. Superstudio, landscape with figures, 1970: montage. Reproduced from Colin Rowe and Fred Koetter, Collage City (Cambridge, MA: MIT Press, 1978), p. 42

Despite its immanent hollowness, monolithic architecture has not altogether overcome the anxiety of the orifice. In this architecture, windows and doorways are still instances of tension that require extraordinary treatment and inevitably deviate from habitual configurations. For instance, in the Signal Box and the Baron Vert, design ingenuity is concentrated almost exclusively in the reinvention of the window. In the Signal Box, the surface revetment is gradually distorted to become permeable, only in strategic locations, in front of traditional windows. In daylight, the windows are barely perceptible behind the visorlike ribbons of copper; at night, because of the artificial lighting behind, they become the dominant feature of the elevation. The building remains impenetrable during the day, whereas its character changes dramatically when the luminescent cavities are exposed in the darkness. Under these conditions, it seems less impregnable, as if its metallic armor has been lifted for congenial nocturnal activities.

The diurnal striptease of the Signal Box is translated into a spatial register in Starck's Baron Vert. The windows of this building are sculpted like a *déchirure* in a stretched fabric, but the gaps are only visible from a certain distance. In the close-up view from the street, the building seems totally opaque, except for a large opening that cuts through the lobby and the opposite wall to frame a cemetery in the backyard.

The veiling of the orifice, whether in screenlike cladding or anamorphic concealment, epitomizes again the ambivalent desires that are enacted in this architecture. The persistent intent is to emphasize the formal integrity and a sense of homogeneity in the building. The unbroken continuity of the surface is a prerequisite for this task. However, there is an investment in program and issues of inhabitation, a commitment to the enhancement of interior environments. Most often, this entails differentiated spatial qualities and modes of occupancy within a single structure: varied light conditions, ventilation, and visual connections to the exterior. In short, there is a need and concomitant desire to break through the opacity of the monolithic surface. With its flickering apertures, monolithic architecture could yield to the informal patterns of everyday life and still maintain the hermetic consistency of its public visage, at least at certain times, from a certain angle or distance.

Contrary to expectations, monolithic architecture is not necessarily predisposed for programs that require very few openings to the exterior such as auditoria, theaters, shopping malls, and department stores. In fact, when no windows are required at all, the architecture has recourse to other devices to expose its vibrant cavities. Hence Moneo's glowing rock. Monolithic architecture would slip into the tranquil banality of the dumb box if its objecthood were not put into crisis by the exigencies of the orifice.

The quotations in this essay were taken from the following sources: Antoine de Saint-Exupéry, *The Little Prince* (San Diego, New York, and London: Harcourt Brace Jovanovich, 1982), pp. 7–8; Patrice Goulet, *Jean Nouvel* (Paris: Electa Moniteur, 1987), p. 106; Philippe Starck, *Philippe Starck* (Cologne: Benedikt Taschen, 1991), p. 25; and Robert Venturi, Denise Scott Brown, and Steven Izenour, *Learning from Las Vegas* (Cambridge, MA: MIT Press, 1982), p. 87.

Paulette Singley

Moving Solids

Embedded within monolithic architecture is the archaic monolith, a freestanding stone saturated with divine powers that is capable of civilizing and disciplining its subjects. Among the various characteristics of the archaic monolith — described, for example, by the menhir, stele, obelisk, or pillar — its lapidary countenance expresses the hard and impregnable visage of a stable, potent, and portentous order: the stuff of which despotic dreams are made. In this totalizing guise, the monolith serves as an inflatable signifier for architecture's phallic economy. Although grown from nature, it is unnatural; although a millennial object weathered by time, it stands a priori and alien to its surroundings — stolen from a "dark continent," fallen from the sky, or erected by unseen forces.[1] When understood as something radically other than its context, the monolith's displacement comprises another characteristic that antedates, as well as enhances, the aspect of its fixity. A paradoxical representation, it must be light enough to lift and move, yet it must ultimately appear too heavy to budge even the slightest millimeter. Moreover, the mechanism of its transport has long been assimilated within the monolith's mute form, one of the encrypted secrets that forces its meaning to circulate within an open linguistic field. Indifferent to racial, sexual, and semantic distinctions, the monolith is a signifier that floats, oscillates, and doubles upon itself into that very form of instability which its undisputed authority purportedly resists. As a variant of this archaic predecessor, the architectural monolith has mutated from solid stone into polished walls whose prismatic silhouettes conceal heterogeneous interiors. Despite this physical change, it remains an arrested body that stalks our apprehension of the object. Thus, the levitation I will attempt in this short essay will be to demonstrate the means by which the monolith impresses itself on our architectural unconscious so that we dream of it as floating, walking, and even reproducing. This approach assumes that figural sculpture mediates between monolithic architecture and the human physiognomy as an avatar of the automato: an avatar that hypothesizes a "mechanomorphic" assemblage of flesh, stone, and metal, constructed at the intersection of petrified eroticism and the desire for a cybernetic body.

The Primal Scene

On close inspection, the veiled phallus painted on the wall of the Villa dei Misteri at Pompeii, the one that inspired Jacques Lacan to consider phallic signification as similarly concealed, can be seen to have been rendered with a flat top. Given that its anatomical reference is described through a rectilinear shaft rather than

a close approximation of the male organ, the object is veiled not only by cloth but also by lithic abstraction. Although it would not have been possible to witness Saturn severing the paternal penis, ancient Greeks might have been able to see Uranus's castrated member fall out of the sky, land in the sea next to the island of Cyprus, and emerge from the bubbling foam as the goddess Aphrodite. Later worshipped in the form of a black meteorite, or Baetyl, as George Hersey has narrated, the stone idol of the goddess in her temple at Paphos referred to these phallic origins as well as to her heavenly body.[2] With Aphrodite's local appellation of Paphia, meaning "bubble up" or "foam," the Baetyl reproduces both masculine weight and feminine buoyancy as a generative episode of the monolith's ability to float above the predictable gender distinctions that would describe it as a specific representation of the male organ.[3] Both a castrated male fragment and a phallicized female body, the monolith's fall and subsequent rise rehearses the primal trauma of architecture's dangerous and ambiguous investment in the body, demonstrating that it is not as easy to translate sexual difference into abstract form as one might wish. Furthermore, Hersey has explained that columns portraying the male organ, called *phalloi*, were set up in front of the temple at Paphos and that other such *phalloi* were carried in processions or erected throughout Greece.[4] At once solid, impregnable, immutable, immovable, virile, and penetrating, the monolith also signifies something porous, mutable, portable, fertile, and uterine: the castrated male transformed into the phallic female.

A similar myth of origins locates the term *colossus* in equally precarious a position as the monolith's anthropomorphism and concomitant sexuality. The Coliseum, its name a malaprop applied to what rightly should be referred to as the Flavian Amphitheater, received this sobriquet due not to its magnitude, but rather to its proximity to the 120-foot-tall statue that was known as the Colossus of Nero. Furthermore, in its original Greek usage, *colossus* referred not to size, but to the concept of a simulacrum, a substitute image or representation. In this sense, the statue's impersonation of Nero, rather than its size, classified it as colossal. As Jean-Pierre Vernant has clarified, in earlier episodes of the colossus's mythic history "the word conveyed nothing about size" and did not "refer to effigies of gigantic, 'colossal' dimensions as it later came to do for purely accidental reasons."[5] Vernant has explained that in ancient Greece, *colossoi* were life-sized substitutes for absent bodies of either gender which referred to "a peculiar and ambiguous presence" that was simultaneously "a sign of absence."[6] Quite specifically, when someone died and the corpse could not be located, a body-double was devised in order to prevent the *psuché*, or spiritual double, from wandering among the living and causing trouble. Similarly, when a spouse died or was absent for a prolonged period of time, a colossus might be used as a substitute partner. In either case, whether the colossus filled the sepulchral or the matrimonial chamber, it did not reproduce the specific features and details of the human body, but instead stood in as a crudely formed idol constructed of rough-hewn stone, wood, wax, or other such available materials. While the colossus of a deceased person claimed a direct link to the underworld, the associations of colossoi used in magic concerned with love also conveyed an otherworldly message. As a stand-in for an absent spouse, the *colossus* would fill the gap in bed and substitute for the object of desire to such an extent that it would be possible for the present partner to make love to the effigy.[7] Likewise, when news of the dead was received from a foreign messenger, the master of the house would make one colossus of a man and another of a woman and then welcome these abstract guests to his table and offer them food. Once the rites of hospitality were completed, the colossoi were taken to an uncut wood and planted in the ground.

Unlike other "portable idols," such as the *xaonon*, that "were moved from place to place, [or] carried in processions," the dominant characteristic of the colossus was its immobility.[8] And yet, despite the necessity for fixity that would root the wandering double in a single spot, there was, as with the heavy monolith, an argument for its mobility; it had to be light enough to be carried to bed and to tumble with its corporeal lover.[9] Although Vernant insisted that "by embedding the stone in the ground, the intention is to fix, immobilize, localize in one definite spot of the earth, this elusive *psuché* that is at the same time everywhere and nowhere", this fixedness referred not to something that cannot, but rather to something that should not, move.[10] And while it was the *psuché*, not the idol itself, that threatened to roam, statues and effigies often were bound, chained, or fixed in ways that would alleviate this anxiety of mobility.[11]

Simultaneously a fallen projectile, amorous stone, and ersatz body, the monolith emerged from the birth of Aphrodite and her subsequent engagement with the colossus as an unformed object flung from the heavens that bore some vague resemblance, as both part and whole object, to the human body. From the consanguinity of Aphrodite's Baetyl, the body-double, and the archaic monolith arose lithic forms that screen an anthropomorphic projection upon architecture that is independent of precise verisimilitude.[12] The geometric abstraction that constructs this anatomical analogy offers a preliminary criterion for approaching the architectural monolith that would describe the Kursaal Cultural Center and Auditorium as a lapidary shard sunk into the earth on which it has landed; the Walloon Forestry Department Shell as a tethered dirigible half-submerged in the ground; the New National Theater in Tokyo as biceps pumping iron; the Baron Vert tower as a vertical wing suspended above the ground; and, similarly, the T-House as cantilevered wings frozen in ascent. Although this floating imperative might also apply to those precarious exercises of revolutionary Russia exemplified by the Lenin Institute (see Wang, fig. 2), Palace of Culture, or Wolkenbügel, the architectural monolith is not constrained by a similar demand for structural or programmatic transparency; form and content are allowed to flow past each other and sometimes to intersect. To summarize, from Aphrodite's lofty origins and the colossus's approximation of human anatomy, the architectural monolith surfaces as a brute stone planted firmly in the ground, a body-double independent of direct mimesis, or a fallen object that aspires toward its spatial origins. Its fixity and proximity to the earth gesture toward aerial mobility.

Venus redivivus

When the goddess of love weds the colossus in bed, they produce the legend of "Venus and the Ring," a story that displaces the deity from her temenos, garden, or museum pedestal and locates her precisely in the nuptial chamber. The earliest known version of this story, from twelfth-century England, tells of a Roman bridegroom who places his wedding ring on the finger of a statue for safekeeping. On trying to retrieve his precious possession, he finds that the statue will not release it from her bronze hand. Later that evening, he climbs into bed with his new wife and senses something "dense and cloudlike" between them that whispers: "Embrace me, since you wedded me today. I am Venus, on whose finger you put the ring, and I shall not give it back."[13] Unable to consummate his marriage, he resorts to sorcery in order to liberate himself from Venus's charm and to initiate conjugal relations with his bride. These events — the placing of the ring on the statue and her subsequent animation in bed — remain constant throughout the legend's literary vicissitudes.

Dense yet cloudlike, the statue's impenetrable vapor forms a physical impediment, which, as Theodore Ziolkowski has observed, rationalizes sexual impotence.[14] It is an impotence, I should add, constructed on female virility. The reciprocal forms of the groom's ring and Venus's extended finger describe a transsexual union of female body-as-phallus and male body-as-womb wherein the statue comes alive while the groom becomes flaccid and lifeless. The statue must remain petrified and immobile in order for the male member to perform similarly. Insofar as the statue's stiffness metonymically reproduces the desired response in the male body, this dualism of female virility and male impotency suggests a psychoanalytical exigency to the colossus's fixity that obliquely mirrors the myth of Medusa. While Medusa's powers of destruction and her subsequent decapitation refer to castration anxiety, her petrifying gaze allays this fear as an embodiment of phallic stiffness.[15] In a perplexing modification of this myth, the legend of "Venus and the Ring" directs Medusa's gaze away from the fetish as substitute object and onto the analyst, appearing in the role of sorcerer, who cures the patient and restores sexual prowess. In contrast to the petrification-castration dyad, the stories of Venus and other walking statues suggest the alternative construct of animation-obstruction which refers specifically to the architectural monolith. While it is tempting to inscribe the Medusa myth upon the monolith as a part object — translating it into an assemblage of Perseus's sword and shield that has the power to capture reflections and to split subjectivity — as a whole object, it amplifies, as well as mitigates, an anxiety of virility rather than castration. The monolith is both an animated object whose relative magnitude renders the subject impotent and a petrified object that reconfirms potency. Likewise, while the monolith stands as a physical obstruction between the viewer and the world, interior and exterior, it nonetheless beckons the physical or visual penetration that its solidity supposedly denies.

Dense yet cloudlike, Venus's apparition beckons toward the monolith hovering among Max Ernst's images of floating women, severed limbs, and barometric spheres. Ernst positioned the female anatomy in an intertextual landscape in which disembodied hands place the set pieces of a metaphysical game onto an aerial board. When rendered into the montage novel of *La femme 100 têtes* (1929), the legs of Alexandre Cabanal's *Birth of Venus* float out of their foamy origins and into a nineteenth-century science experiment (Fig. 1). It is precisely the technique of montage, the cutting and pasting, which floats the image on its background and similarly floats the monolith, as a foreign object, onto the surface of its context. Such buoyancy refers specifically to the floating balls that inhabit Ernst's work and evoke the vulnerable images of globes, eyes, eggs, balloons, breasts, or testicles, images that capture the ambiguous nature of the architectural monolith as it appears in the work of Boullée and Ledoux, as well as the eighteenth-century fascination with spatial solids.[16] The "atmospheric" solids of the Cenotaph to Newton or the House of the Agricultural Guards at Maupertuis refer to celestial origins as well as to earthly captivity; at once dense and permeable, opaque and transparent, light and heavy, these forms disturb architecture's telluric hegemony (see Wang, fig. 1; Mertins, fig. 4).

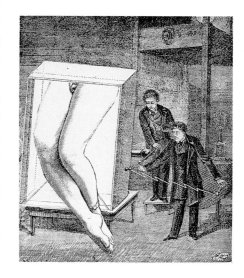

Fig. 1. Max Ernst, La femme 100 têtes, 1929: ". . . and the third time missed." Reproduced from Rosalind Krauss, The Optical Unconscious (Cambridge, MA: MIT Press, 1993), p. 79.

Fig. 2. Max Ernst, At the First Clear Word, 1923. Reproduced from Rosalind Krauss, The Optical Unconscious (Cambridge, MA: MIT Press, 1993), p. 69.

Venus's crossed legs morphologically reproduce the disembodied fingers in Ernst's mural *At the First Clear Word* (1923), in which the sphere appears on a feminine hand and directs this discussion back to the walking statue (fig. 2). The mural alludes to the wall paintings of Pompeiian houses and serves as a topographical reference to the Surrealist's fascination with Freud's *Delusion and Dream in Jensen's Gradiva* (1907). In *Gradiva: A Pompeiian Fantasy*, Wilhelm Jensen tells the story of a young archaeologist who escapes his sexual repression and bachelorhood by projecting the image of a woman's feet, depicted in an ancient bas-relief, onto the body of a childhood sweetheart named Zöe. Upon encountering Zöe in Pompeii, he fails to recognize her as anything other than the wandering eidolon he has named Gradiva. It is only through the living woman's complicity with her role as an incarnation of the long-dead Gradiva that the archaeologist is cured of his delusions and is able to welcome matrimony. In this warped version of the Venus myth, the woman's body progressively transforms from stone and death back to flesh and blood as the man regains his own phallic power. Despite the reversal of stone into flesh, where animation results in penetration, the statue's ability to walk nonetheless concerns the monolithic relationship between stone and virility.[17]

When Ernst transcribed this story into images, Gradiva's legs became fingers that balance a ball tied to a string. Rosalind Krauss's analysis of this mural enucleates the monolith from this sac:

> The hand, indescribably languid, was wholly suggestive, its crossed fingers turning the tender web of flesh at the fingers' base into a beautifully folded crotch, the feminine source of what could now be read as two voluptuously dangling legs. But it wasn't just the transformation of hand into "woman" that caught his attention. The ball, you see, pushed things further than that. The verticality of the fingers with the ball at their tips rephallicized the image, causing a meaning to rise upward, to flood back over the lineaments of the baffling genital secret; in it he could see the woman's body beckoning with all the pleasure and terror of the dawning excitement of the experience of sexual difference.[18]

Within this array of crossed fingers, tender flesh, folded crotch, and dangling legs, Krauss described the ball's presence as a visual discourse that caused meaning to "rise upward." This is the condition of the monolith as an inflatable signifie: it is capable of maintaining the precarious balance of physiognomic ambivalence that Ernst captured in the intersection of balls and fingers. As meaning rises upward, the monolith serves as a psycholinguistic shifter that floats, like a retinal afterimage, in front of our eyes.

The Stone Guest

Insofar as "the two walking statues most famous in Western culture are no doubt those in the stories of Pygmalion and Don Juan," as Ziolkowski has suggested, the story "Venus and the Ring" falls into a category of legends concerned not only with the act of creation and the vivification of inert matter but also with the act of seduction.[19] Furthermore, the walking Venus also leads to Romanticism's "curious fascination with the phenomenon of automata."[20] When transferred into the legend of Don Juan, Venus is split between the Don's powers of seduction and the dead father's powers of animation such that the libertine bachelor replaces the counterfeit bride in bed, and the Commendadore's statue replaces her on the pedestal. Recalling that Moliere and Mozart derived their versions of Don Juan, in part, from Tirso de Molina's *El Burlador de Sevillea y convidado de piedra* (The seducer of Seville, or the stone guest 1630) — which, in turn, was based on a legend dating from late medieval Spain — despite the many differences between these narratives, each tells the story of a statue that "walks." In the more famous versions, the statue of a Commendadore, who has been killed by the Don in an effort to avenge his daughter's lost virtue, accepts an invitation to dinner and sends the unrepentant libertine to an infernal tomb. As suggested by the subtitle of Molière's play, *The Stone Feast*, the story of Don Juan refers directly to the rites of hospitality surrounding the Greek *colossoi* and to the survival of superstitions that concern the living feeding the dead. Once again, phallic power is on the table, for in refusing to eat, the Commendadore sustains his appetite for a vengeance that can only be satisfied by the Don's living body. Given that Don Juan's "mythic death stems from a dinner invitation," as Shoshana Felman has suggested, "the hermetic subtitle of Moliere's play . . . refers to the stone of the statue itself as a concrete image of death, not only as that which breaks the meal, but as that which, by definition, cannot be digested, assimilated, or understood."[21]

In this form, then, the monolith would similarly stand as an indigestible stone interrupting the architectural banquet. But what precisely are the festivities that it interrupts? Felman has explained:

> If myth, in general, is an allegory of history, the Don Juan myth may become specifically an allegory of the way in which history at once *makes* itself and gives itself to be *misunderstood*: an allegory of the stone banquet. If the *stone* of the feast is in reality what history cannot assimilate — what is indigestible in the language of the feast . . . — it is also, at the same time, the very stone that makes — or builds — history, the stone that although unassimilated, is nevertheless the *cornerstone* of history.[22]

The Stone Guest's and the monolith's presence at the banquet, then, is a modern example of the colossus's ability to wander. It also is an example of modernity's resistance to incorporating the historical imperative of tradition that the Commendadore embodies. Likewise, it exemplifies postmodernism's inability to assimilate modernity's patricide. In this sense, it reveals the monolith to be the unassimilated cornerstone of architectural history. The Commendadore further allegorizes the tacit relationship between stone and death that thematizes the concrete box of the Baron Vert tower hovering over a field of tombstones.

Given that the Don's corporeal, and hence flaccid, sword is no match for the statue's impenetrable body, we have here the dichotomy of penetration: obstruction describes the once virile Don as impotent in a story in which stone remains the master of discourse.[23] Likewise, the confrontation of expert seducer and intractable statue locates the monolith at the center of a quarrel — between ancients and moderns, patriarchy and transgression, subjugation and liberty, tradition and innovation, age and youth, impotency and virility, and so on — that distills these mutual antagonisms into architectural discourse. Architecture in this sense must either conform to the dictates of an established order or it must shatter this order to pieces; in either case, it reifies the existing institutional hierarchy within the mausoleum of history. When, it would seem, only two such choices are available, the monolith enters as a third term that emulates what it subverts — a simulacrum of order that symbolizes its very absence.

In an architecture divided between libertines and nightwatchmen, the Commendadore's stone statue approximates the monolith more closely than does the body of the frivolous Don. However, if the revolutionary also stands guard, then it is possible to expose the monolith as a spy in a higher service, a member of the secret police, or a dialectical seducer. This is precisely the description that Theodor Adorno arrived at regarding the protagonist of Søren Kierkegaard's *Diary of a Seducer*. [24] In assimilating Don Juan into the *Diary*, Kierkegaard removed the statue, but rehabilitated the Commendadore as a figure of authority who also happened to be a nefarious bachelor. Kierkegaard offered an alternative to the Don's murder/suicide that transformed the dilemma of aging into a seductive advantage. Old enough to be the girl's father, yet young enough to finish the job, Kierkegaard's seducer methodically follows and stalks his naive prey until she succumbs to his wisdom and experience. This critique of the Don's artless and inconsistent technique parallels Kierkegaard's similar conclusion in *Either/Or* (1843) that the Don is not a calculating seducer, that, as Adorno wrote, "he does not prepare tactical maneuvers" but is an "excellent improviser."[25] Stalking is the operative word in this story that Georg Lukács described as conveying "an incorporeal sensuality and a plodding programmatic ruthlessness."[26] The dialectical seduction Adorno referred to would demonstrate the possibility that, between the playful and amateurish Don, the merciless and unflagging Commendadore, and Kierkegaard's professional seducer, the police might enjoy subversion as much as the seditious might enjoy discipline. Kierkegaard's seducer demonstrates the value of patience, experience, history, and partriarchy, of following societal strictures in order to undermine them.

The list that tallies the Don's 1,003 acts of seduction transforms the seducer into an animated mechanism; no longer entirely human, he is a machine driven by powerful psychological forces. Insofar as Lacan treats Don Giovanni as an example of the repetition compulsion, this drive to complete an infinite list is what defines the legendary lover as an *automaton*.[27] Similarly, Michel Serres has written:

> A statue is an art object or a ritual icon. In the classical era it also becomes an automaton, an anatomical model, a laboratory device, a mechanical model of the living being. Condillac models his imaginary experiment after a statue, and before Condillac there is the Cartesian Robot. The Commander's statue is a machine, Don Juan's death a machination.[28]

With Serres's analysis, the Don Juan legend moves from describing a confrontation between stone and sword into one in which the intersection of flesh and metal approaches F.T. Marinetti's dream of the body as an erotic war machine. With Marinetti, the tide of the battle turns once again in favor of youthful virility and metal tropes as the phallic signifier that could defeat the ancien régime of marble statues. This epistemological break was constructed on the juncture of a petrified eroticism — the love of stone bodies sublimated within Winkelmann's noble simplicity and calm grandeur — and modernity's libidinal preoccupation with machines — described as the body's dreamt-of metallization.

This antipathy between modernity and mythology, of course, is not entirely fluid. As an "unholy coupling of the atavistic and the futuristic," the monolith synthesizes the desire to incorporate both stone and metal. Indeed, it is the same "unholy coupling" that Terry Eagleton defined as fascism, and with this return of the secret police, the monolith once again ventures into a suspect political camp.[29] But it does this as infiltrator rather than interrogator, reappropriating forms that have been under attack: those singular, minimal, and bare geometries that have been synonymous with authoritarian regimes, the forms that Fredric Jameson has described in terms of paranoid vision: "[T]he glass skin repels the city outside; a repulsion for which we have analogies in those reflector sunglasses which make it impossible for your interlocutor to see your own eyes and thereby achieve a certain aggressivity and power over the Other."[30] If the monolith's reflective visage engenders it with aggressive power, the dissimulation of Kierkegaard's seducer invests it with subversive authority; if the monolith wears dark glasses and the well-cut uniform of a seducing machine, it nonetheless undermines the preconceptions of power which such images project; if the monolith assumes the capacity of a phallic signifier, it does so as a curiously desexualized object.

A metallized body foreshadowed by the bronze Venus, the monolith, too, stirs from its archaic slumber as an ominous and androgynous union of metal and stone which gestures toward a mechanized future through the mythological past of its *Ur-Suppe*. It is a petrified body that stalks and seduces its prey with unflagging, if imperceptibly slow, motion. It is an object that frustrates assimilation or digestion while it swallows the subject in its shadows and reflections. It is a lapidary solid constructed, with sharp precision, at the intersection of myth and science. Characterized by a disturbing anthropomorphism, it evokes the image of disembodied armor or a mechanized hulk. It reveals itself in the tonsured giant of the Sea Terminal, its bubble helmet rising up from the ocean floor; in the motile legs of the Max Reinhardt Haus, swerving toward an ominous engagement; in the cyclopean visage of the Signal Box auf dem Wolf, a spotlight threatening to transform silhouettes into captives. These monoliths initiate the recurrent nightmare of a technology that cannot arrest what it has created, of a mechanical incubus that offers a premonition of buildings, like animated statues, that walk when we sleep, of a somnambulatory architecture that seduces with assiduous determination. It is an avatar of the future based on a more primitive epistemology, and while it might be a fragment that has fallen up from a primordial landscape, it itself is not fragmented.

Artificial Reproduction

In what might have been an historical coincidence, Mozart's *Don Giovanni* was first performed in 1787 in Prague, the city of the Golem. Given that these two legends center on the theme of walking statues, there must be more than geographical proximity between the Golem and the Commendadore. From ambulatory statues and the latent anthropomorphism of even the most amorphous stone to fantasies of mechanized bodies and artificial spouses, the Commendadore and the Golem embed themselves in the architectural monolith as reproducible terms. The legend of the Golem concerns an artificial being, designed to be either a servant or an instrument to protect the Jews from pogroms, that later turns on its creator and wreaks havoc among the community. It is the allegory of the architect-engineer giving birth to her or his own means of destruction and the fear that the creation will be able to reproduce itself. In particular the story directs the architectural body and the ethics of creation — gene splicing, parthenogenesis, artificial insemination, and genetic engineering — into the monolith's fertile form.[31] As a shell that houses disparate contents, the architectural monolith compresses within its swollen body those smaller contents that threaten to burst forth from the slightest cesarean incision. These little beasts float peacefully in the amniotic continuum of space, feeding off the infrastructure of the parent building and depositing a second level of signification into the monolith's ability to float.

In a sculptural group titled *Rock Drill*, Jacob Epstein depicted an androgynous driller that contains an unborn fetus within its ribbed torso (fig. 3). Epstein's own description of the piece offers a concluding set of observations on the architectural monolith:

> It was in the experimental pre-war days of 1913 that I was fired to do the rock drill, and my ardor for machinery (short-lived) expended itself upon the purchase of an actual drill, second hand, and upon this I made and mounted a machine-like robot, visored, menacing, and carrying within itself its progeny, protectively ensconced. Here is the armed, sinister figure of today and tomorrow.[32]

Fig. 3. Jacob Epstein, The Rock Drill, 1913. Reproduced from Richard Buckle, Jacob Epstein Sculptor (Cleveland: World Publishing Co., 1963), p. 67.

The fetal torso and the penetrating drill externalize the latent physiognomy of Aphrodite at Paphos, wherein the male and female principles merge into a hybrid monster. The simple form of the driller — its streamlined torso, structural ribs, and helmeted head — is itself a small monolith that, when amplified by the colorful terminology of "ardor for machinery," "machine-like robot," "visored," and "menacing," miniaturizes the characteristics of the larger architectural monolith. The violence of the driller, metaphorically shattering the sculptor's medium of stone with its metal rod, reveals the narrative of the artist's mutilation of his medium. Once again, metal prevails over marble. Most important, Epstein specifically referred to the monolith's capacity for reproduction when he described it as "carrying within itself its own progeny." Such reproduction appears in the twin blocks of the Kursaal Cultural Center, where two complementary polygons indicate the serial mutation of a fraternity planned "in vitro." Conversely, the vehicles moving within the parietal volumes and tubal spaces of the Yokohama International Port Terminal indicate a conception planned "in utero." Although the terminal evokes the image of waves washing over a foundering ship, the gentle undulations of flexible diaphragms, of layers that regulate and simulate flow, also form a titanic landscape of swollen and stretched skin. Through its precise geometry, crisp silhouette, and simple forms, the monolith appears to be a product of the larger mathematical sequence that anticipated its construction. Likewise, if Epstein's progeny represents a latent reproduction endemic to all machines, then it is not necessarily a literal birth that describes the monolith, but rather its ability to spawn similar formal experiments. In other words, like the machine that carries future iterations within its functional defects, the monolith, too, rehearses improved variations through its technological imperfections. As an object that is petrified in motion, the monolith is an architectural illustration of Lessing's famous proclamation that sculpture should represent the "pregnant moment" of an episode. What this means is that architecture, like sculpture, should depict the moment leading up to a crisis or catastrophe rather than the catastrophe itself. Finally, given that the archaic monolith is embedded within monolithic architecture, this abstract stone inseminates the modern monolith with a more primal ontology.

In terms of the initial adjectives describing the architectural monolith — hard, impregnable, stable, potent, and portentous — in more recent variations, potency and portentousness seem to be its only invariable features. Its atmospheric visage undermines its hardness, its tumescent silhouette suggests that it is pregnable, and its equivocal status as a phallic signifier describes it as fundamentally unstable. As a gestating as well as inflatable signifier, the monolith inserts itself into our subjectivity as an embryonic object; initially simple and ordered, it grows and doubles upon itself into a full-blown abstraction of the human body. Although not necessarily large, it dwarfs; although not actually "conceived," it challenges our conceptions; although not really capable of motion, it moves us to perceive it as such. In other words, while the architectural monolith may not exactly be capable of walking in its sleep, it is certainly capable of walking in ours.

1 Jane Gallop has written: "'Dark Continent' is a term Freud used for female sexuality, a term frequently quoted in French psychoanalytical works ('continent noir'). I have not yet succeeded in locating this term in Freud's text, but that may be my blind spot" (*Reading Lacan* [Ithaca, NY: Cornell University Press, 1985], p. 127). In Rome alone, where I happen to have written this essay, there is ample evidence of the necessity for the monolith to be movable and floatable. The obelisks and columns that were taken from Egypt on ships and the marbles that were transported up the Tiber from distant quarries were not guaranteed fixity. Dominico Fontana's 1590 treatise *Della transportatione dell'obelisco Vaticano*, about moving the obelisk from Nero's circus to its present location in the piazza in front of St. Peter's, is a compelling description of the necessary portability of monuments and the fascination with the mechanism of their mobility.

2 On the Temple of Aphrodite at Paphos, see George Hersey, *The Lost Meaning of Classical Architecture: Speculations on Ornament from Vitruvius to Venturi* (Cambridge, MA: MIT Press, 1988), pp. 47–52. Here, Hersey reiterates that "Saturn quarreled with his father Uranus, cut off the paternal penis, and flung it into the sea off Paphos. When it hit the foam it turned into Aphrodite"(p. 47). Adopting a slightly different version of the story, Jennifer Bloomer has written: "Melancholy is the attribute of Saturn, or Cronos (who castrated his father and brother, Uranus, birthing Aphrodite from the blood [PHARMAKON]), the dualistic god of extremes. One of the forgotten symbols of melancholy, Benjamin points out, is the [STONE], which is also . . . an allegorical emblem par excellence" (*Architecture and the Text: The [S]crypts of Joyce and Piranesi* [New Haven: Yale University Press, 1993], pp. 51–52).

3 Hersey (note 2), p. 52.

4 Ibid., p. 49.

5 Jean Pierre Vernant, *Myth and Thought among the Greeks* (Boston: Routledge, 1983), p. 305. I am grateful to Matthew Fisher for pointing me toward Vernant's observations regarding the monolith. I also am indebted to Anne Marie Davis, whose continued enthusiasm about the Coliseum has infiltrated this essay.

6 Vernant (note 5), p. 307.

7 Ibid., p. 305. Among the examples of the colossus as a surrogate spouse, Vernant summarized an event from Euripides's *The Protesilaus*:

> Protesilaus meets his death near Troy, in a faroff land, and his body cannot be brought back to his fatherland. He leaves behind him an inconsolable widow. In the version of the story given by Apollodorus, the wife, whose name is
> Laodamia, makes an ειδωλον of her husband. Each night she makes love with this double. The gods take pity on her and send the psuché of Protesilaus back to his loving wife for a moment [p. 310].

8 Ibid., p. 305.

9 In his novel, *The Blue of the Noon*, Georges Bataille introduced Don Giovanni's Commendadore as a spectral vision. Denis Hollier analyzes this story and describes Bataille's interest in burial as "a committing to an abyss into which the earth tumbles as the entombment takes place." Richard Miller's translation note informs us that "Tombe, tombeau, tomber — grave, tomb, to fall, come down, abate, and so on — [are] the verbal acrobatics "that resound in the grave upon which Bataille wrote" ("Bataille's Tomb," *October* 33 [Summer 1985], pp. 73–74).

10 Vernant (note 5), p. 313.

11 The wings of the statue of Athena Nike were removed in order to prevent the goddess from abandoning Athens and, as Vernant mentioned, the effigy of the dead Actean was chained to its site in order to prevent his spirit from wandering (ibid., p. 313). Theodore Ziolkowski has offered an additional explanation for chaining statues:

> The belief in animated images occurs most frequently in religious contexts. Many ancient peoples — the Egyptians, Sumerians, Jews, Babylonians, Indians — believed that the statues of their deities were animated by the incorporation of the god in the image. For this reason these peoples liked to steal the divine statues of their enemies in order to benefit from the virtue inherent in them. Numerous stories for other cultures attest to the religious belief that statues come to life. Thus we hear of a Burmese statue of Buddha that grew a mustache. In Japan, statues of Jizo walked about at night in disguise. In Scandinavia, a statue of Thor talked and even wrestled with warriors. The Spartans chained down their statue of Ares, just as the Thryians shackled their image of Baal, lest the deities desert their city [*Disenchanted Images: A Literary Iconology* (Princeton: Princeton University Press, 1977), pp. 21–22].

12 As Vernant has written:

> [T]he material substance no longer resembles the form of a living body in its previous appearance; rather, it replaces the form of a radical

otherness from its actual being, just like one of the dead. The marker attests to the strangeness of the deceased's status in the world beyond, of his exile into another realm where all the realities here on earth are inverted. The stone is cold, hard, dull, opaque, rough crude, and fixed as the young and living body is warm in the heat of the sun, supple, brilliant, luminous in its gaze, soft to the touch, and nimble and mobile in its movements [ibid., p. 89].

13 Ziolkowski (note 11), p. 18.

14 Ibid., p. 27.

15 As Freud interpreted the myth of Medusa, "to decapitate = to castrate." Insofar as Medusa's terror was a fear of castration linked to vision, this fear "occurs when a boy . . . catches sight of the female genitals . . . surrounded by hair" and discovers the missing penis. Both the head of Medusa and the vulva are apotropaic objects to the male gaze: when openly displayed, they produce a feeling of horror or petrification in the male viewer. I am grateful to Daniel Bertrand Monk's important unpublished work on apotropaism for directing me to this passage in Freud's analysis of the Medusa myth. See Sigmund Freud, "Medusa's Head," in *The Standard Edition of the Complete Psychological Works of Sigmund Freud* (London: Hogarth Press, 1953).

16 Rosalind Krauss's *The Optical Unconscious* (Cambridge, MA: MIT Press, 1994) has been instrumental in developing the concept of the floating monolith. Regarding Ernst's balls, she noted "their obvious allusion to the part object: the breast, the eye, the belly, the womb" (p. 81).

17 In usurping Jensen's position as author within his own analysis, Freud monumentalized a charming, but somewhat insignificant novella. Gradiva has been handed down through diverse interpretations, from André Breton and André Masson's Surrealist allusions, through Sarah Kofman and Anthony Vidler's interpretations of the uncanny, across Hélène Cixous and Jean Baudrillard's critique of psychoanalysis, to Victor Burgin's photographical essays and Emily Apter's concern with the fetish object. See Breton, *Communicating Vessels*, trans. Mary Ann Caws and Geoffrey T. Harris (Lincoln, NE: University of Nebraska Press, 1990), vol. 1; Masson, *Evolution of Gradiva*; Vidler, *The Architectural Uncanny: Essays in the Modern Unhomely* (Cambridge, MA: MIT Press, 1992); Burgin, *Formations of Pleasure* (London: Routledge, 1983); Apter, *Feminizing the Fetish: Psychoanalysis and the Narrative Obsession in Turn-of-the-Century France* (Ithaca: Cornell University Press, 1984); Verena Andermatt Conley, *Hélène Cixous: Writing the Feminine* (Lincoln, NE: University of Nebraska Press, 1984); and Baudrillard, *The Ecstasy of Communication*, trans. Bernard Schutze and Caroline Schutze (New York: Columbia University, Semiotext(e), 1987).

18 Krauss (note 16), p. 68.

19 Ziolkowski (note 11), p. 29. Ziolkowski has written:

Rousseau's monodrama Pygmalion (written 1763; performed 1770), generated a singular new theatrical fashion that lasted for about forty years: the "attitudes." These attitudes — the 'mimoplastic art' of representing works of art by mimic means, especially gestures and draperies — were essentially the creation of one woman, Emma Hart, the subsequent Lady Hamilton . . . The bizarre conceit of representing "living statues" is simply another example of the late eighteenth-century obsession with statues: with statues *per se*, with statues that come to life, with people who turn into statues, and with the ambiguous relationship between people and statues. During the 1780's for instance, it was vogue in Italy to visit the galleries at night in order to view the statues by torchlight, which produced the illusion that the statues were alive and moving [ibid., pp. 34–35].

20 Ibid., p. 35.

21 Shoshana Felman, *The Literary Speech Act: Don Juan with J.L. Austin, or Seduction in Two Languages* (1980), trans. Catherine Porter (Ithaca: Cornell University Press, 1983), p. 54.

22 Ibid., pp. 144–45.

23 The confrontation of the Don with the living father, which results in the Commendadore's death, adheres to Felman's interpretation of the story as a "seduction" that occurs in the etymological sense of that word as "to separate." She also has seen the second confrontation occurring between the Commendadore and the Don in Molière's version as the confrontation of two cutting metals, "Time's scythe and Don Juan's sword" (ibid., pp. 43, 45). I, however, see the second confrontation as the impotency of metal to penetrate a stone ghost; the relevant law battles between phallic order and sexual anarchy, father and son, seduction and repulsion, love and death.

24 Theodor W. Adorno, *Kierkegaard: Construction of the Aesthetic*, trans. and ed. Robert Hullot-Kentor (Minneapolis: University of Minnesota Press, 1989). Adorno referred to Kierkegaard as "a spy in a higher service," "part of the secret police," and "a dialectical seducer" (p.11).

25 Søren Kierkegaard, *Either/Or Part I: Kierkegaard's Writings III*, ed. and trans. Howard V. Hong and Edna H. Hong (Princeton: Princeton University Press, 1987) p. 101; Adorno (note 24), p. 13.

26 As cited by Adorno (note 24), p. 6.

27 Lacan wrote: "I would ask you to re-read Kierkegaard's essay on *Repetition*, so dazzling in its lightness and ironic play, so truly Mozartian in the way, so reminiscent of *Don Giovanni*, it abolishes the mirages of love" (*The Four Fundamentals of Psychoanalysis* [1973], ed. Jacques-Alain Miller, trans. Alan Sheridan [New York: Norton, 1978], p. 61).

28 Michel Serres, *Hermes: Literature, Science, Philosophy*, ed. Josué V. Harari and David F. Bell (Baltimore: Johns Hopkins University Press, 1982), p. 3.

29 Terry Eagleton, *The Ideology of the Aesthetic* (Oxford: Basil Blackwell, 1990), p. 348.

30 As cited by Jacqueline Rose, "Sexuality and Vision: Some Questions" (1984), in Hal Foster, ed., *Vision in Visuality: Dia Art Foundation Discussions in Contemporary Culture Number 2* (Seattle: Bay Press, 1988), p.116. As Rose has written about this quotation, "One of the things that strikes me about these images, however, is their curious desexualization, or rather the way that this absorbing of sexuality into the visual field closes off the question of sexual difference"(p. 116). In his novel *The Blue of the Noon* (1934–35), Bataille arrived at an interpretation of the Commendadore that placed him in an ambivalent position between Jameson's description of aggressiveness and power and the potential for overthrowing that very order. Regarding this ambivalence, Denis Hollier has asked if Bataille's interest in the Commendadore should allow us to posit a sympathy for fascism ([note 9], p. 90). Hollier responded that the Commendadore represents a revolutionary figure, that there is a Marxist version of the Commendadore (ibid., p. 94).

31 On the ethics of artificial reproduction in relation to the Golem, see Byron L. Sherwin, *The Golem Legend: Origins and Implications* (Lanham, MD: University Press of America, 1985).

32 As cited by Richard Buckle in *Jacob Epstein Sculptor* (London: Faber and Faber, 1963), p. 98.

Detlef Mertins

Open Contours and
Other Autonomies

Closed yet open, inert yet elastic, abstract yet figural, the contours of the examples of monolithic architecture included in this exhibition are surprisingly permeable and mutable. Asserted and denied, the simplicity of these forms is mitigated by material and surface gestures, partial transparencies and internal uncertainties, producing effects that exceed any strict, stable, or singular delineation of the object. Hybrid, contradictory, and paradoxical, these uncanny objects suggest that the oppositional logics that have served to structure Western thought have lost their efficacy, especially those that contour the edges of architecture to maintain the symbolics of order and disorder, inside and outside, reality and dream. Instead, the fusion of realism and fantasy, familiar and alien, that these projects embody asks for a performative understanding both of the matrix of normative practices that regulate the production and reception of buildings, and of how it is possible to elide, overflow, or possibly even transform this matrix.

To position the elusive contours, shifty surfaces, and open interiorities of monolithic architecture in relation to twentieth-century modernisms and minimalisms, I will consider these works as objects — free-standing, striking shapes charged with identities, logics, or ideas that promote recognition while remaining ambiguous and indeterminate. Looking again at the architectural object as a locus of identity, in full recognition of the critiques of autonomy and self-determination which have been made over the past decades in architecture (as in cultural theory) leads almost inexorably into the discourse of architectural autonomy, for which the independent block has often served as a privileged signifier. The tension and movement between identity and uncertainty, known and unknown, that these figures provoke in the viewer bring into legibility their various tactics for pushing at the permissible limits not only of what constitutes the architectural object but also of what architecture takes its normative domain to be. One of the distinguishing conditions of monolithic architecture is that these projects draw on the visual arts, popular culture, science, and technology in ways that expand this range.

A cosmopolitan ensemble, monoliths cannot be treated monolithically and resist efforts to assimilate their singularities into a canon. But perhaps they will allow themselves to be considered as testimonies of the struggle for architectonic identity today — its problematics, multiplicities, instabilities, and potentialities. Understood as re-enacting the body (or bodies) of architecture, monoliths may open up earlier conceptions of architecture to pleasures, doubts, and possibilities beyond their boundaries, perhaps beyond the capacity of conception itself. For the very gestures that delineate them as objects also produce powerful effects of estrangement — experiences of difference borne by constructions of identity. Consequently, the following readings oscillate between bringing old positions on

autonomy to these objects and reading them in their specificity as forms and artifacts that materialize new positions.

Contours

Jean Nouvel's entry for the New National Theater competition (1986) — in collaboration with Philippe Starck — begins to set the terms. Invoking Albert Einstein — "the most beautiful thing we can experience is the mystery of things" — the architects' descriptions of this extraordinary object mobilize the language of effects and correspondences to suggest ways in which the building exceeds itself. As Nouvel has written, "Our project is a monolith of polished black granite that contains three precious objects. A great shining stone that acts as a mirror for the sky, the city and the people. A building that 'shows' ... or 'conceals' the mystery it contains, thus recognizing itself as a magic object."[1] For Starck,

> It's a strange object which has come from somewhere else, it's the whale that swallowed Mecca. Object and non-building, huge dimensions, formidable weight, you'd say it was made of solid marble: the weight of a black hole. Inside it, there's only symbol and drama, emotions, great passages — suspended organs like stomachs and livers, an obvious animal reference to emotions. Yes, the order is impressing: the emotional gift that I give people is the gift of living an impressive moment, of experiencing a certain dimension, a weight, almost an anxiety — standing in front of a huge object, beyond comprehension.[2]

Like the case of a musical instrument, the membrane of an organ, or the protective shell of a machine, Nouvel's solidity is hollow, but not empty. Or perhaps the hollowness of its Piranesian interior marks an indeterminacy and splendor that lighten the weight of civil society, opening up its worldly pomp and spectacle to unnerving winds from alien places. A primal, fleshy imagination pushes and tugs — like something repressed that never goes away — from within the rationality of the minimal block, deforming and inflecting the familiar calculus of minimum enclosure for maximum internal volume. Elastically, the building's skin stretches around the upper theaters and into a kind of expressivity which makes the everyday impenetrable and the impenetrable everyday. Bounded but boundless, familiar yet tense, whole and fragment, enigmatic and unassimilable, the building visibly eludes itself, failing to hold its shape as it enters an expanded field of correspondences with other things, known and unknowable.

That the body of architecture should need to reconfigure its contours from time to time has been a condition of the relentless drive of technological modernization to render norms obsolete. Nineteenth-century theories of modern tectonics wrestled with the question of how to draw new industrial materials and processes of production, together with the unprecedented needs of mass society, into systems of architectural representation as they had been conceived for construction methods in earlier eras. But for all the dexterity with which theorists such as Carl Bötticher, Gottfried Semper, and Eugène Viollet-le-Duc reset the terms of artistry in the context of modern means, many disconcerted voices complained that frame construction, be it in iron or wood, was simply unacceptable for architecture, since it lacked surface. More precisely, since it lacked the expressive surface of stone. For instance, in the words of the German critic Karl Scheffler, writing as late as 1908, with iron construction "there is no mystery" for there is "no mass, no surface." Mass and surface were key because the artistic handling of construction "aims at something soulful and fashions a body for this soulfulness with the means of artistic forms that express this inner force."[3] Yet, a few years earlier, Alfred Gotthold Meyer's treatise on iron constructions had already celebrated the new steely beauty of the sublime Eiffel Tower (1889) along with the new sense of breadth, height, and space made possible by engineered iron structures, especially bridges and the great halls of the late nineteenth-century international exhibitions.[4] It was the soul-shattering power of structures like the ethereal Crystal Palace (1851) and the robust Galerie des Machines (1889) — their ability to achieve effects of infinite expansion and lightness — that finally demanded legitimacy for the new body of iron and glass architecture, having appeared as if naturally, or magically, from the blast furnace of the earth — raw, colossal, skeletal constructions without flesh, appearing outside the matrix of social attention, born of that peculiar marriage between rationality and imagination that so ignited the nineteenth century — the age of X-rays, no longer certain of boundaries (fig. 1).[5]

Of course, Nouvel's black case is still a child of the Industrial Revolution, whose inventions were refined over the course of the twentieth century as they were being superseded in their role of forging new realities by revolutions in media and information technology. But significantly, Nouvel's project converted into opacity the transparency of early modern architecture, not only the literal transparency of glass but also the physiognomic transparency associated with the rational shaping of matter into technical structures or self-identical primary forms (elementarism). Rather than restaging these, Nouvel mobilized large spans and suspended volumes in concert with techniques of concealment (offering only glimpses), transmutation (polishing, coating, plating, and encasing), and metamorphosis (stretching, bulging, swelling), thereby staging a mimetic play of similarity and difference.

Fig. 1. Victor Contamin and Ferdinand Dutert, Galerie des Machines, Paris, 1889. Reproduced from Sigfried Giedion, Bauen in Frankreich, Bauen in Eisen, Bauen in Eisenbeton (Leipzig: Klinkhardt & Biermann, 1928), p. 54.

Theater

At the other end of the spectrum of size, Simon Ungers and Tom Kinslow's tiny T-House (completed 1992) is similarly expansive and unfathomable, but achieves these effects through the concreteness of its abstraction. While the tactility of abrasive, rusting surfaces and the obdurate rigor of geometric solids could not be further from Nouvel's sensuous optical seductions, even here things are not unequivocal. For once again, the autonomous opacity of the building's mass is corroded by externalities, not only through weathering but also by the inscription of the subject. In Constructivist terms, the subject is inscribed by the building's elemental expression of its internal program of uses; in Minimalist terms, by the dependency of its identity on the perceptions of observers moving in relation to it like actors in space; and in the terms of contemporary theory, by its circulation in the space of culture. For, no less than in Nouvel's black box, and in keeping with its pedigree in the "objecthood" of Minimalist sculpture, the formalist quest for pure, self-critical self-sufficiency is inadequate to Ungers and Kinslow's T. On the one hand, a mechanically regular repetition of incisions opens the surface of objectivity to the engagement of the subject, providing glimpses of inner mysteries from the outside and panoramic vistas from the inside. On the other hand, the building's form is sufficiently composite to elude easy identification; someone approaching from the road would need to move onto, into, and around it in order for its gestalt to crystalize, not instantaneously, but synesthetically, which is to say never completely. Then again, this seemingly abstract geometrical form is vaguely anthropomorphic, more precisely zoomorphic, not so much returning empathetic projections (which aim to fuse subject and object into a psychic unity) as looking back at the viewer with an alien and unassimilable gaze. The obvious transposition of forms and materials from Minimalist sculpture (especially works by Richard Serra) into building corrupts the presumption that each discipline drives itself to the limits of its competency, and at the same time heightens the "theatricality" of architecture. The building's existential surfaces provide platforms against which the enactment of life is obliged to take its own measure. And by assuming the guise of Minimalist sculpture, the T paradoxically stages self-reflexive and self-determined autonomy more effectively than if it had remained within the conventional means of architecture, although it was precisely the absoluteness of this autonomy that Minimalism sought to qualify as contingent.

To sort out the relationship of the T-House to Minimalist art, on the one hand, and to the modernist striving for objective limits on the other, I would like to review Michael Fried's efforts to distinguish between modernism and Minimalism in his much-discussed essay of 1967, "Art and Objecthood," which structured much of the subsequent debate around Minimalism itself.[6] Fried's point of departure was the explicitness with which Frank Stella, Robert Morris, and Donald Judd distanced themselves from what he took to be modernist painting and sculpture. "The literalist case against painting," Fried wrote, referring to Morris's insistence on working in literal rather than pictorial space,

Fig. 2. Tony Smith, Die, 1962. Courtesy Paula Cooper Gallery, New York.

> rests mainly on two counts: the relational character of almost all painting; and the ubiquitousness, indeed the virtual inescapability, of pictorial illusionism . . . Above all they are opposed to sculpture that, like most painting, is "made part by part, by addition, composed" and in which "specific elements . . . separate from the whole, thus setting up relationships within the work."[7]

A modernist aligned with the European tradition that Judd and Stella eschewed,[8] Fried's point of departure for his essay was necessarily defensive, and his arguments were critical, looking to discredit Minimalism by revealing its internal contradictions and exposing its detrimental implications for modernist art and for the arts as such. For Fried aligned himself with Clement Greenberg's conception of Modernism as the relentless critique of each discipline's medium and characteristic methods, "not in order to subvert it but in order to entrench it more firmly in its area of competence" through a relentless process of purification, "eliminat[ing] from the specific effects of each art any and every effect that might conceivably be borrowed from or by the medium of any other art."[9] Not only is Fried's essay, then, a defense of modernist painting and the kind of modernist sculpture that Greenberg had promoted in his essays of around 1960,[10] but it reinforces and elaborates Greenberg's critique of Minimalism. Fried's defense, then, marks a complex negotiation between terms used by the Minimalists to distinguish their works and those developed by Greenberg and himself. Thus, where Greenberg held that painting must be pictorial and not literal, the Minimalists contended that art should not be relational, but should occupy the same space as the spectator and strive toward objects that were single, whole, and indivisible, shapes that were constant, known, and "just there," unitary type-forms giving rise to strong gestalts (fig. 2). But by accepting the Minimalists' self-construction on one side of a binary opposition that was not always the same as Greenberg's, and by then taking up the challenge to defend the other side, Fried's argument was unable to effectively address the flow, exchanges, and dependencies between the two "positions," as well as the tendency for inversions and reversals that inevitably accompanies such efforts to constitute a position by excluding its opposites, exclusions that thereby assume a constitutive role.

Consider, for instance, Fried's various discussions about parts and wholes. Anthony Caro's exemplary Modernist sculptures resist being seen in terms of objecthood, for they consist in "the mutual and naked juxtaposition" of the various metal elements that make up the work, "rather than in the compound object that they compose." It is "the mutual inflection of one element by another, rather than the identity of each" that is crucial, and it is this syntactic understanding of how meaning operates that "makes Caro's art a fountainhead of antiliteralist and antitheatrical sensibility."[11] Acceptable for the internal structure of a work, it was precisely the structural principle of relationality and contextuality — introduced into modern art by Cubism[12] — that Fried objected to when it was transferred by the Minimalists to the literal and concrete space that art shares with the observer, the space of apparent immediacy. By insisting on the wholeness and irreducibility of the object, by reducing it to an elemental, plain, and hollow unit, the Minimalists foregrounded that object's relationship to beholders, other objects in space, and space itself. While staged, these relationships (as Robert Morris pointed out) could not be fully controlled, as had been the case with pictorial relationships.[13] Fried's insistence on the autonomy of the arts revealed a profound fear of losing art as such, once its operation in "real" space had been recognized — a fear that severed him not only from the Minimalists but also from the heterogeneous body of European modernism which sought to extend or revise Cubism into a fully environmental program, be it Constructivist (Malevich, El Lissitzky), Elementarist (Mondrian, van Doesburg), Expressionist (Taut, Gropius), or Purist (Le Corbusier). At the same time, however, it also masked the recurring bias of Greenbergian formalism toward a universal two-dimensionality, regardless of medium.

Or consider, as another instance, the apparent contradiction in Fried's characterizations of "objecthood" and "theatricality," terms he used to explain one another. While in discussing theatricality he suggested that the object includes the beholder and is incomplete without him or her, in introducing the notion of objecthood he called on Greenberg's observation that Minimalist works have a certain kind of presence made possible by endistancing the beholder from the object, opening up and sustaining a gap between them through the object's relative size, shape, and location as well as its hollowness, which endows it with a mysterious persona. Where Fried thought he had uncovered a fatal inconsistency in the anthropomorphism of this kind of stage presence — for Morris had explicitly rejected the anthropomorphism he had recognized in the gestures of Caro's elements — it is precisely such weak corporeal similarities that activate the play of identity and nonidentity, resemblance and difference, which establishes the space between subject and object so important to the theatricality of Minimalism's objecthood. That Fried's binary logics — art/non-art, pure/impure, autonomous/contingent — were unable to register the importance of such mutualities for the effects of self-estrangement necessary to the self-critical modernist tradition is a measure of the extent to which Greenberg's modernism had isolated itself from the breadth of the very tradition it sought to promote.

Interestingly, Fried did not attempt to refute the allegation of anthropomorphism in modernist art, but chose instead to expose it in Minimalism, too. Nevertheless, he did attempt to *deflect* the charge when, in discussing Caro's sculptures, he suggested that they "defeat, or allay, objecthood by imitating, not gestures exactly, but the *efficacy* of gesture; like certain music and poetry, they are possessed by the knowledge of the human body and how, in innumerable ways and moods, it makes meaning."[14] That is to say, for Fried, modernist art operated not in imitation of the body, but phenomenologically, on and in relation to the perceptual conditions of corporeal knowledge. Like the formalists and empathists of the turn of the century, who likewise attempted to reground art and architecture in what they understood to be bodily cognition,[15] Fried's case for the autonomy of art (which may be considered separately from his case for the autonomy of *the* arts) aimed at the preservation of a refuge from the everyday world for transcendental aesthetic experience, capable of "secreting or constituting a continuous and perpetual present." He concluded that "We are all literalists most or all of our lives. Presentness is grace."[16] Clearly, then, the distinction between modernism and Minimalism that Fried insisted on was not between autonomy and heteronomy, the self-criticism of artistic practices and the phenomenology of perception, but between different attitudes toward the relation of art to society — its publicness or privateness — which in turn structured their respective attitudes toward the subject-object relation, autonomy, construction, convention, and beholding.

For many years, the art critic Rosalind Krauss has explored the strategic historical importance of Minimalism, which she defended first by turning Fried's critique of theatricality in its favor, and more recently by resisting its absorption into the dematerializations of the abstract sublime.[17] Navigating a course that has avoided the pitfalls of conceiving the thing-in-itself alternatively in the language of bounded purity or boundless dissolution — the beautiful or the sublime — she has insisted on the art object's contingent status within the grid of perceptual, cultural, and institutional externalities that mediate its production and reception, on the very theatricality that Fried feared. In recent writings that strive to safeguard Minimalism from appropriation by those who, like Jean-François Lyotard or Count Panza di Biumo, have tried to assimilate it to the sublime, Krauss has argued that Minimalist works such as Stella's striped paintings and Morris's "L-beams" (to mention only a few) forced the issue of contingency into the open — "the permeability of both subject and object to what goes on in the space in which both coexist." By thematizing the role of context in terms of the perception of the viewer, by staging the subject's experience of contingency, Krauss has contended that this moment in the 1960s set the stage for "widening the 'space' of interaction [between subject and object] to include all those matrices — language and media — which both precede and exceed the bounds of the individual" and for understanding the coordinating matrix to "include the institutional construction of that very 'space': the legal and financial 'arrangements' that shape and control it; the discursive practices that make possible what can become visible within it."[18] That these matrices are themselves contingent explanatory constructs operating within the loop of mutual mediation that characterizes subject/object interaction gives special significance to works that postulate models for these constructs as they strive to overflow their boundaries. Agnes Martin's grid paintings and Cindy Sherman's citational portraits have both been mentioned by Krauss as exemplary in this respect.[19]

Fig. 3. Robert Morris, Columns, 1961–73. Painted aluminum, each 96 x 24 x 24 in. Reproduced from Rosalind E. Krauss, Passages in Modern Sculpture (Cambridge, MA: MIT Press, 1994), p. 202. Photo: Bruce C. Jones, courtesy Leo Castelli Gallery, New York.

If, for Krauss, Morris's paired aluminum *Columns* (1961–73; fig. 3) possess a kind of stage presence, their apparent formal identity differentiated as well as animated by their respective orientations in relation to the viewer — one vertically erect, the other horizontally prone —then Ungers and Kinslow's welding together of two such "columns" into a more complex compound figure, their inhabitation of its hollows for a kind of existential domesticity, their insertion of it (like Serra's steel plates) into a sloping landscape and its location within the renewed culture of abstraction in contemporary architecture as in art — all of these qualities elaborate this theatricality precisely by blurring the oppositional distinction between Minimalism and Modernism as portrayed by Fried. Combining the wholeness, hollowness, and presence of objecthood with a relational syntax, the T demands an expanded understanding of contextual contingency, such as Krauss suggested is available in poststructural cultural theory — expanded to include the Minimalist debates, as well as exchanges among the arts. That Ungers and Kinslow's monolith plays with tropes common to the rhetoric of self-representation among the arts — with planar surfaces, insistent materiality, and irreducible blocks — that it begins in rational reduction and the self-disciplining pursuit of limits, but ends in their transgression, displays the theatricality of resistance, the sensuality of asceticism, and the operative — potentially transformative — role that abstraction and autonomy can play within representation.

Surface

By focusing attention once again on the correspondences between the bodies of objects and those of viewers — in Krauss' words, by "counting on how we sense through our own corporeal selves the meaning of this represented gesture, of that sculpted stance" — Robert Morris called the bluff of modernist sculpture as holding up "a mirror of fixed, stable forms, models of rationality, of organic coherence, of technological mastery."[20] Not only did his sculptures show that there are bodies on both sides of that mirror; they also foregrounded how bodies and objects alike "surface-into-meaning," how meaning occurs on the external plane. Yet, if Minimalism could be characterized for Krauss through this "worry about surface, about the interface formed by materials as they stretched across the frame of either painting or three-dimensional object, aligning the meaning of the work with its physical medium, as that medium 'surfaced,' contingently, into the world," such worries were not entirely new to the history of modern art and architecture, although previously they had been seen to be problematic rather than constitutive. In fact, anxiety about the contingency of bodies on the physicality of surfaces had reached acute levels during and immediately following World War I, when art and architecture, repelled by the devasting experience of that war's destruction through modern technology, reacted against the Cubist and Expressionist fragmentation of bodies and objects into semiotic and prismatic fields by mobilizing once again the well-contoured objects of classicism and realism. Considered more broadly, this "return to order" and the classical tradition — marked also by primitivisms, elementalisms, metaphysicalisms, and critical realisms — may be understood as continuing prewar responses (avant-garde as well as conservative) to the ongoing destabilization caused by progressive industrialization and its capacity to dissolve all that is solid — including the human body and objects of worldly existence — into air. While for some the ethereal atmosphere of the

Galerie des Machines, like an Impressionist painting, was sublime, for others the aesthetics of disintegration signaled descent into chaos.[21]

In France, a return to classicism that could be considered avant-garde rather than reactionary had already become prominent through major post-Impressionist exhibitions around 1904–7, including showings of the work of Cézanne, Seurat, and Gauguin. This work was distinguished from conservative and academic classicism by a freer attitude toward formal invention, taking classicism not so much as a given body of forms, tropes, or exemplars, but as a search for essentials. Operating in tension with the experiences of modernity, this combination of classicism and radical abstraction had become evident by 1920 in paintings by Picasso, Braque, Gris, Derain, and Léger, and also became the explicit basis on which the Purists Amédée Ozenfant and Charles-Edouard Jeanneret launched their re-ordering of Cubism in 1918 to accord with aesthetic principles they hoped would link antiquity, the Renaissance, post-Impressionism, industry, and scientific theories of perception. Although they valued Cubism's rational compositional logic, they rejected its dismemberment of objects and figures, for, as they wrote, "a face is, after all, a plastic continuum."[22] Their concern for the universality of intelligibile concepts and aesthetic experiences led them to render everyday objects, such as bottles, glasses, plates, and guitars, as having physical integrity and weight while subjecting them to the structural principles of the flat canvas and the two-dimensional surface of the retina.

A few years later, in attempting a similar "return" for architecture, Jeanneret — now writing under his architect pseudonym, Le Corbusier — was obliged to confront the contingency of mass on surface, given modern methods of construction. While seeking to adapt architecture to new social, economic, and technological conditions, Le Corbusier nevertheless insisted on the plasticity of primary geometric forms, arguing historically that they emerge "inevitably" in "the process of materializing naked facts" and contending that "their concurrent capacity to arouse emotions, to move the observer" is essential to distinguish the art of architecture from utilitarian engineering.[23] The universal value of cubes, cones, spheres, cylinders, and pyramids was, for him, a direct consequence of their power to move everyone — the child, the savage, and the metaphysician alike.[24] But he worried about the vulnerability of hollow modern constructions to the overworking of surfaces with false ornamentation, as well as over-perforation with apertures in response to the utilitarian need for communication between inside and outside. For architecture to remain "the masterly, correct and magnificent play of masses brought together in light," Le Corbusier warned, "the task of the architect is to vitalize the surfaces which clothe these masses, but in such a way that these surfaces do not become parasitical, eating up the mass and absorbing it to their own advantage: the sad story of our present-day work."[25] This meant that those holes and transparencies that were "often the destruction of form . . . [had to] be made an accentuation of form."[26]

Le Corbusier's identification of pure, elemental, or absolute forms as architecture's distinctive means was indebted to Peter Behrens's neo-Kantian pursuit of a priori forms in neoclassical and geometric elementarism, begun in 1904–7, while he was director of the influential Düsseldorf school of decorative arts, and continuing into his designs for the AEG company, during which time, Jeanneret worked in his Berlin office.[27] The link between Le Corbusier's much-read polemics for pure form and the neo-Kantian discourse of autonomy was identified by the Viennese historian Emil Kaufmann in his 1933 prehistory of architectural modernity, *Von Ledoux bis Le Corbusier* (From Ledoux to Le Corbusier). It was Kaufmann's book that first proposed a pre-twentieth-century neoclassical origin for architectural modernity as a project of autonomy aligned with the critical philosophy of Immanuel Kant.

Since completing his dissertation in 1921, Kaufmann had focused his research on the forgotten struggles of Claude-Nicolas Ledoux and his contemporaries in late eighteenth-century France to free architecture from all manner of external determinations (including the styles of previous eras) and reground it strictly in its own rationality. In his book, however, Kaufmann interpreted these efforts as parallel and homologous to struggles in other spheres of culture and society and sought a level of recognition for Ledoux and the project of self-constituting architecture that would be comparable to that already afforded Kant's critical path in philosophy, the political philosophy of Jean-Jacques Rousseau, and the revolutionary *Sturm und Drang* movement in German drama. On the assumption that these parallel manifestations of spirit were mediated by the internal nature, logics, and rules of each medium of expression — from lived politics to architecture and literature — Kaufmann assigned a manifold of formal and qualitative properties to architectural autonomy. Amalgamated from various architectural writings, including those of Le Corbusier, Adolf Loos, Richard Neutra, and Gropius and the Bauhaus, Kaufmann singled out free-standing cubic blocks, unadorned surfaces, windowless walls, flat roofs, pure forms, Ur-forms — prismatic building elements that were the physiognomic expression of their inner purpose, objective, sober, lawful, necessary, and moral; assembled part by integral part into composite buildings, themselves arranged in the manner of independent pavilions, into "republican" urban ensembles. But while these characteristics could, on the one hand, be understood as inherent in the discipline itself (to architecture-in-itself), their service as figures and metaphors for the rhetoric of autonomy, individualism, republicanism, and revolution is so clear, and so clearly a formalization of these nonarchitectural ideas, that the paradox of Kaufmann's literary dependencies for his conception of autonomous architecture becomes evident.

Yet, despite the absolutist tone of Kaufmann's claims, he considered the project of self-governing reason to remain necessarily incomplete and unfulfilled.[28] For within the neo-Kantian tradition, heteronomy and organicity were taken to be conditions not only of premodern architecture and society (especially the "absolutist" totalizations of the Baroque), but of humanity itself, requiring the continual re-enactment of the passage from childhood to maturity, which Kant used to portray the idea of Enlightenment. Notwithstanding this final acknowledgment of the contingency of pure forms as representations of autonomy, it was Kaufmann's solid cube — the paradigmatic, stereometric stone block having become stone once more, *sachlich*, even *nüchtern* — that provided the dominant image of modernist autonomy in architecture until its displacement by Colin Rowe's mathematical and striated interpretations of Corbusian Purism in the 1950s and '60s. Or, perhaps of even greater symbolic importance, it was Ledoux's spherical House of the Agricultural Guards of Maupertuis that became emblematic of "absolute" architecture. Certainly, Hans Sedlmayr, also an historian of the Viennese School, focused on this image in his conservative response of 1948 to Kaufmann's republican interpretation of Ledoux's modernity, taking the sphere house to be symptomatic of nihilistic tendencies in the modern era, the era of decentered and foundationless "autonomous" individuals (fig. 4).[29]

Fig. 4. Claude-Nicolas Ledoux, House of the Agricultural Guards of Maupertuis: perspective view. Reproduced from Emil Kaufmann, <u>Von Ledoux bis Le Corbusier, Ursprung und Entwicklung der Autonomen Architektur</u> (Stuttgart: Verlag Gerd Hatje, 1985), p. 31.

Intimations of a purist and elementarist conception of autonomy had already appeared in the prewar writings of the architect Ludwig Hilberseimer, marked by his close reading of Le Corbusier. In the conclusion of his *Großstadtarchitektur* (Metropolitan architecture), published in book form in 1927, he rendered this conception in language that combined the self-determination of neo-Kantianism with the organicism of Goethe and Weimar classicism as well as the "absolute" of German romanticism. Without invoking the notion of autonomy directly, Hilberseimer wrote of a new, self-fashioning architecture striving for clarity, logic, and inner truth, of a metropolitan architecture forging its own forms and rules that would be the necessary and objective expression of a new feeling for life. Insisting on "an architecture formed exclusively from itself," he nevertheless described how it was research in painting that brought the fundamental forms of all art into recognition — "geometric and cubistic elements that do not permit of any further objectivization." And in a not uncommon vulgarization of Kant's unrepresentable notion of the thing-in-itself, he assimilated certain representations to it, suggesting that an architecture "based solely on its most primitive and [formative] elements" would be composed of "cubes and spheres, prisms and cylinders, pyramids and drums." These, he continued, "are the foundational forms of every architecture. Their corporeal definitiveness compels order to come into formal clarity, brings order into chaos in the most realistic way."[30]

Fig. 5. Ludwig Hilberseimer, Blumenthal House, Berlin-Zehlendorf, 1932: street view. Courtesy Art Institute of Chicago.

It is a sign of the curiously shifting character of the autonomy discourse in architecture that Kaufmann dropped the term *autonomy* as well as references to Kant from his writings after his arrival in the United States, replacing them with a more distinctively American insistence on "individualism." Hilberseimer, on the other hand, having followed Mies from Berlin to Chicago in 1938 to teach at the Armour Institute (later Illinois Institute of Art), not only incorporated Kaufmann's interpretation of Ledoux's Ideal City in his later writings on urbanism, but in his 1964 history of modern architecture drew the major movements of modern architecture together under the title "Towards an Autonomous Architecture" — Le Corbusier's "revived Classicism," Russian Constructivism, Dutch Neoplasticism, German Expressionism, and the "structural" architecture of Mies himself.[31] "The architecture of the 'Twenties," Hilberseimer wrote,

> was characterized by its objectivity, its directness, and its simplicity. Its trend was toward architectural autonomy. It aimed to free itself from all external influences, from all traditional bonds, to be self-determined, and to realize its goals by the true means of architecture. It tried to discover the elements of architecture and to use them in their purest form. Not all of the architects of the 'Twenties attained this aim. But some even went beyond it and brought architecture back to the realm of art — a rare achievement![32]

In striking contrast to the sureness and fullness of Hilberseimer's prose, his architectural projects reveal a profound unease, seemingly about the very forms advanced in the writings. Where he alluded in the latter to strong founding forms, his cubic elemental houses, such as the Blumenthal House in Berlin (1932; fig. 5), seem so brittle and empty — so thoroughly devoid of Le Corbusier's plasticity, sensuality, and emotions — that they undercut the founding gesture of the pure form. Instead of substance firmly anchored to the ground, the tautly stretched enclosure of the Blumenthal House is staked tenuously on the surface of existence. The size and proportion of the windows, like the size and proportion of the rooms, appear stingy, minimal, and utilitarian, their locations often pushed uncomfortably close to the edges, their blankness marking the equally blank surfaces of the walls with a palpable tension. Drawings for unrealized projects convey similar qualities, or a similar absence of qualities. Schematic line drawings using dramatic perspective angles emphasize architectonic outlines rather than material properties. Highly contrasting shadows and blackened window openings make the volumes seem haunted and abandoned.

Radical in the self-alienation of their abstraction, extreme in their rationalist denial of empathy, Hilberseimer's projects are depleted of the kind of psychic investment or subjective interiority commonly associated with dwellings. Instead, following Dada's merciless critique of the hankering for soulful expression (characteristic of Expressionism's staging of bourgeois subjectivity), Hilberseimer's schematization brought the dwelling into line with the reduction of individuality in mass society, considered valid under industrial collectivism as well as under bourgeois capitalism. But where capitalism sought to compensate for the alienation of labor and the resultant reification of objects in the exchange economy by reapplying the signs of individuality, tradition, and myth, these designs by Hilberseimer reject the projection of such "fullnesses" and instead demand that the empty surface be confronted in its stark reality, cut off as it is from the meaning-context of its making and maker, its capacity for surfacing-into-meaning undercut by the system of commodification. What is evident in the work, but remains untheorized, is that Hilberseimer was mobilizing a schematic rendering of a priori form, not as an essentialism per se, but as a registering of the effect of industrialized mass society in separating life from form. Where for Nietzsche, a work of art without the Dionysian intoxication of life became decadent and enfeebled, Hilberseimer's withered Apollonian impulse to order undermined the normative expectations of bourgeois art for fullness, strength, and vitality and at the same time made a virtue of proletarian impoverishment, operationalizing its potentiality, as in the sketches of Heinrich Zille or in Walter Benjamin's meditation on the potential of impoverishment for social reinvention.[33]

On the surface, Jacques Herzog and Pierre de Meuron's elemental *and* tectonic, schematic *and* vitalized, Apollonian *and* Dionysian, a priori *and* phenomenological Signal Box auf dem Wolf (completed 1994) could not be more different from Hilberseimer's shrivelled one-dimensional cube. Yet, it too elides the comfortable projections of bourgeois subjectivity, of wholeness and self-sameness, its surfaces materializing the geometric as corporeal in a kind of self-estranging architectural objectivity. By wrapping, or more properly coiling, the utilitarian concrete box with horizontal, partially twisted copper bands, swaths of darkness and shadow open up at the same time that light passes between inside and out. It is as if the impressionable naïveté of the building had been brushed by the passing of a dark force. And while the crisp corners of the autonomous block stand sharply against its setting, the surfaces loose their definition and capacity for containment. Soft, textured, diaphanous, porous, even breathy, their partial transparencies combine seduction and the stiff flexibility of a venetian blind. Here, the self-representation of the object's interiority on the exterior surface remains incomplete, its identity mysterious, just as its similarities remain inadequate for assimilation into the already known, its difference profoundly estranging, and yet entirely captivating, mesmerizing, holding a kind of unnameable promise.

Where Herzog and de Meuron twisted open the surface of the autonomous block, no longer willing or able to repress the corporeal and relational conditions that such autonomy had tried to exclude — enacting instead the impossibility of self-grounding in the face of the uncontrollable and unknowable unconscious — Philippe Starck constructed the surface of his Baron Vert (completed 1992) as if it had been cut by a knife. Appearing to bend in reaction to the stimulus received, Starck's project evokes Lucio Fontana's cutting of tautly stretched painted canvases, releasing the space within the canvas, as well as the violence of attempting to delimit the painting in space. By allowing the fleshy corporeality of the surface to free itself from repressions that aim for an unattainable transcendence, and then stretching it into a towering pyramid, providing a space for the body by exaggerating its thickness and deflecting gazes by polishing its voluptuous contours, Starck's deformation of the facade as painted surface — like the metamorphic objects of the Surrealists — discharged the anxiety associated with interiority into a space beyond, in which the imagination travels lightly.

The differences between the Baron Vert, the Signal Box, and Hilberseimer's nameless cubes, considered as objects constituted by their physical surfaces, may be understood in relation to distinctions made by the art historian and critic Franz Roh, who coined the term *magic realism* in 1924–25 in grappling with the potent brew of realisms — naturalist, critical, magical, and sur-realist — then emerging in Germany, Italy, and France.[34] At the time, Roh, a student of Heinrich Wölfflin's binary formal analytics, managed to effectively distinguish Post-Expressionism from Expressionism — suggesting, as Wilhelm Worringer put it, that Expressionism had grown cold — but was unable to distinguish among the various positions within Post-Expressionism. In his later history of German art in the twentieth century, however, he explained that he had introduced the notion of "magic realism" to describe a direction different from the neutral realism that Gustav Hartlaub had labeled Neue Sachlichkeit (New Objectivity), also in 1925, and that magic realism sought "an approach to the autonomous sharpness of objects, as in the late Middle Ages, the quattrocento, or the revolutionary form-hardening classicism of David, or Ingres."[35] With its emphasis on abstraction rather than empathy, magic realism also tried to build a bridge to science by revealing something of the wonder of objects materializing as such, the process of becoming and forming from the inchoate mass of substance, which is perhaps what Roh meant by magic, for he was explicit in not taking magic "in the religious-psychological sense of ethnology," setting it instead against myth. For him, the objects of magic realism held mystery behind the surface of objectivity rather than letting it circulate in the world as myth.[36] "If all matter," he wrote, "consisted in minute abstract particles intrinsically in motion, then it was declared to be astonishing, even miraculous, that given such fluctuations, matter should crystallize and solidify into what we can call things." Turning from form per se to the mysterious process whereby form materializes, magic realism emphasized that "the thing, the object, must [continually] be formed anew," that its static, anti-dynamic form was but a coordinate of the "rigid fourth dimension with which modern physics can reduce dynamics to states of being." One of the characteristics discussed by Roh in his survey of Post-Expressionism was the creation of a new sense of space, a double sense that he contrasted not only with the atmospherics of Impressionism, which melded distances together, but also with the graded, planar spatiality promoted by Adolf Hildebrand, which likewise collapsed space into the self-identicality of the surface's flatness. In magic realism, Roh described the astonishing effect of depth produced by joining the extreme polarities of near and far, as well as large and small, while clearly delineating the contours of objects.[37]

Fig. 6. Giorgio de Chirico, <u>Self-Portrait</u>, 1925. Collection Giovanni Deana, Venice.

Roh's terms for magic realism — even to this conjoining of near and far in the surface — seem remarkably apt for the Signal Box, as they do in different ways for Hilberseimer's architecture, which recent interpretations have placed in relation to paintings by George Grosz, Otto Dix, Heinrich Maria Davringhausen, and Anton Räderscheidt, considered by Roh as instances of magic realism alongside de Chirico (fig. 6). While Hilberseimer was edging toward the ambivalent neutrality of Neue Sachlichkeit, and Herzog and de Meuron slid into surrealism, they share the predilection of magic realism to "turn daily life into eerie form." However, the realism of Starck's metamorphic Baron Vert, enfolded as it is in dreaming from art to architecture, has its points of departure already one step removed from daily life and is perhaps more fully in flight toward that higher reality (sur-reality) that "none of us had ever seen before, possibly not even in our fantastic dreams." As Roh recalled of the Surrealists, undreamed-of combinations of experiences

> "like snow and thunderstorm, like cyclone and trembling of the earth" . . . emphasized in a sublimated fashion the mystery and insecurity of life as we know it really is if we think beyond the order we accept in everyday life. Their conception was a variation of the demonic vision with which one can at all times confront the harmonious view.[38]

Mimesis

If monolithic architecture may be taken as oscillating between a melancholic perspective on the possibilities for nonrepressive self-constructions of the architectural object and a more optimistic, though not naive, outlook that lightens the issue of identity into an unresolvable play of self and alterity, then the projects by Moneo, Samyn, Eisenman, Moussavi and Zaera-Polo, and Koolhaas included in this volume may be thought to linger longer on the side of lightness, in the bright spots of that zone shared by architecture and nature, rather than in its dark expanses. Instead of opposing themselves to nature or the organic, as Kaufmann's neo-Kantian elementalism did, they thematize the relation between construction, natural form, and natural process in ways once again indebted to, but distinct from, other autonomies within the history of architectural modernism. There have been at least two streams of architectural autonomy that have grounded themselves in nature — one inorganic (that of crystalline mathematical formalism), the other organic (that of *bauen* and *Gestaltung*). These streams participated in the Enlightenment discourse of "rationalist" aesthetics, whose concern for the transparency of meaning focused on the idea of the natural sign — an original, universal language, a direct and unmediated expression free of the uncertainty and contingency of cultural constructions, semiotic language, conventions, theater, and mimesis. The Enlightenment was profoundly ambivalent about the semiotics of the sign, appreciative of humanity's ability to elevate itself beyond immediate experience by means of language, but suspicious of its limitations and its propensity for delusion and error. While the twentieth-century inheritors of the Romantic tradition would take the resolution of this conflict to be possible in the here and now of crystalline environments, eighteenth century German rationalist philosophers, such as Alexander Baumgarten and Gotthold Lessing, held back, preferring instead to project the possibility of an ideal "transparent" state — free of the deceptive opacity of semiotic language and representation — into the future.[39]

The trope of the inorganic crystal, with its organic-seeming process of self-constitution — crystallization — has long served to mediate the threshold between architecture and nature, to legitimize architecture that aspired to the status of nature. Natural yet not organic, geometric yet not artificial, form (*Gestalt*) and formation (*Gestaltung*), object of science and of magic, the crystal has served as signifier for the idea of a second nature, transcendent yet earth-bound, suspended between sameness and difference. Rafael Moneo's Kursaal Cultural Center and Auditorium in San Sebastián (construction commenced 1995) stages such a fluctuation of identity and non-identity in its two autonomous crystalline blocks deformed by the force of their dislocation from the sea, the ground, and the city, belonging to and yet alien from them all. Like Mies's prismatic Glass Skyscraper (1922), paradoxical and quixotic in its monolithic modernity, the assertion and denial of identity is played out not only in the outline of the forms, but once again in surface effects upon which the materialization of these forms remains contingent. But where Mies's assertion and denial of form concentrated on the "rich interplay of light reflections" to achieve a brilliant oscillation of transparency and reflection, Moneo has emphasized the mysterious luminosity and shifting shadows of layered translucent surfaces illuminated from within during the darkness of night. Sinking back into classical meditations of light and shadow, Moneo's surfaces approach the thickness, opacity, and profiling of stone. Doubled, scalloped, scored — almost ribbed or fluted — they follow the trajectory, evident in the developmental series of Mies's skyscrapers, from the unreliable brittleness of transparency to the inscription of a fleshy, tactile opacity into the very profile of the surface, in order to fold and unfold, open and close as the observer moves around the building. Unlike Mies's dark towers, staging the dream of technolgy's apotheosis in the grayness of the gritty industrial metropolis, Moneo's crystals remain close to the ground, rematerializing the body of an architecture that seeks not a transcendence of nature or technology, but a mediated reconciliation. Like the paintings of Agnes Martin, the act of stepping up to Moneo's crystalline walls promises to release a powerful sensation of optical and spatial expansion through the interplay of structures, textures, and changing light, opening the physicality of the surface not to an interior, but to beyond.

In his landmark history of modern architecture of 1928, *Bauen in Frankreich* (Building in France), Sigfried Giedion characterized construction as the expression of life, the mysterious source of new architectures and new forms of living, a kind of automatic writing of society that "served the role of the subconscious," a spontaneous productivity seeking to realize itself under the constraints of artistic conventions.[40] Rather than assimilating the new to the past, as nineteenth-century tectonic theories had proposed to do for iron structures, Giedion was concerned with the progressive development and clarification of new materials and construction techniques, bringing them into self-consciousness as the formal and technical means for architectural expression. His conception of the semiautonomy of an architectural system based in construction reveals how his negotiation of the marriage of organicism and rationalism relied on a kind of objectification akin to crystallization, coming into clarity and visibility — flowing from the subconscious to consciousness: "the product of all sorts of factors — social, economic, scientific, technical, ethnological . . . an architecture may be called into being by all sorts of external conditions, but once it appears it constitutes an organism in itself, with its own character and its own continuing life."[41]

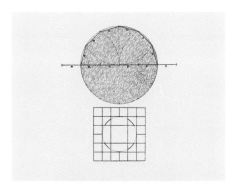

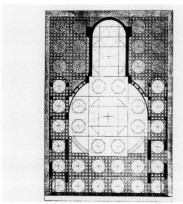

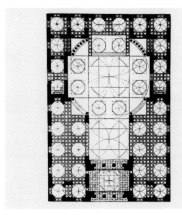

Fig. 7. Demonstration of J.L.M. Lauwericks' system for generating designs using a modular pattern derived from a square with inscribed and circumscribed circles. Project for a church by his student Christian Bayer, published in <u>RING</u> (1904), no. 4.

Like the concrete shell structures of the Swiss engineer Robert Maillart which Giedion so admired, Philippe Samyn's tectonic, translucent, ovoid shell for the Walloon Forestry Department (completed 1995) inserts a refined economy of construction (conceptually, technically, aesthetically) lightly into a given landscape, with deftness, precision, and minimum impact. Here, a rational-expressive deployment of construction both operationalizes and signifies the ethos of husbandry to which the processing of seeds is dedicated. In so doing, it may be considered to extend the dream of a benign and noninstrumental technology, formulated at the turn of the century in terms of a second nature that would result from the unfolding of history and the utopian fulfillment of technology without exploitation or domination. Using technologies at once simple and sophisticated — a double shell of laminated wood trusses clamped to the edges of a concrete slab and clad with layers of tempered Pyrex panels — Samyn's delicately woven mound collapses a century or more of such optimism about construction: from Gottfried Semper's primitivist genealogy of the Crystal Palace in ancient textile-making to Alfred Meyer's sublime portrait of the Eiffel Tower as an open or skeletal body, Mies's early 1920s appreciation of woven industrial structures with skylit roofs, László Moholy-Nagy's mid-1920s architecture of light, and Toyo Ito's electronically modulated Tower of Winds in Yokohama (1986). The curved and undulating planes of Samyn's shell weave a new, more porous and expansive image of the matrix — the architectural object figured as a net that is both mound and womb — just at the moment when the feminist theorist of technology Sadie Plant has argued that computers emerged out of the history of weaving, and that weaving intimates the concealment of the womb, for which the Latin word is *matrix* and the Greek is *hystera*.[42]

Throughout his career, Peter Eisenman has mobilized geometric models and transformational logics in conjunction with theoretical and analytical models from architecture as well as other disciplines in the humanities and sciences, devising procedures whose traces generate, as if automatically, the final form of the project and then remain inscribed and legible in it. For the Max Reinhardt Haus in Berlin (designed 1992), a high-rise office building and cultural center, he drew on the idea of the Möbius strip — a continuous one-sided surface formed by twisting one end of a rectangular strip 180 degrees and attaching it to its other end. Eisenman used computer modeling techniques to produce a mathematical series that transformed the site's shape in response to contextual influences, rotating and changing the shape as it moved along a path defined by the Möbius strip. The shape was not posited to begin with and then graphically modified; rather it was derived entirely from the mathematical formulas. Aiming to achieve a "crystalline form," Eisenman selected certain parameters that stopped it along the path to create planar surfaces, parameters that when changed were able to generate several hundred iterations.[43] By appropriating a formulaic mathematical system, the building appears to write itself despite the deliberateness with which the system itself was constructed and mobilized. And while Eisenman has recently acknowledged the role played by visual and visceral judgment, its exercise in this case remained strictly limited to selecting from among iterations, each of which remained systemically uncompromised.

Unprecedented, Eisenman's generative systems nevertheless emerged out of, and in relation to, his reading of modern architecture, especially the grid structures of Giuseppi Terragni. While comparison with the transformational geometries strategic to Mannerism could also be fruitful, I would like to note the foundational role played by descriptive geometry in the rationalist discourse in architecture since the eighteenth century, and consider the neo-Kantian twist given to it in the geometric experiments of a number of Dutch architects at the turn of the century whose work infiltrated the subsconscious of modern architecture. Analyses by Viollet-le-Duc of the proportional systems used to produce the plans and sections of medieval cathedrals served to legitimize the Gothic in terms equal to those of mathematically regulated classicism and inspired Jan Hessel de Goot, K.P.C. de Bazel, P.J.H. Cuypers, Hendrick P. Berlage, and J.L.M. Lauwericks to work with proportional systems independent of particular styles. Their aim was precisely the generation of a new basis for architecture and new aesthetic effects that would supersede decadent representational practices imitating the styles of previous eras. In presenting the design of a church by one of his students in 1904, Lauwericks described how a modular abstract pattern had been derived from a square with inscribed and circumscribed circles and then used to generate plan, section, and elevation (fig. 7). Consistent with his Theosophical beliefs, Lauwericks took this congruence to signify the achievement of a fundamental unity of form and universal harmony. Stark linear perspectives of the strange and unprecedented form produced by this procedure translated the abstract construct into the image of a not-quite-physical building.[44]

When, in the years following his successful move from painting into the decorative arts and architecture, Peter Behrens abandoned the free-flowing lines of Jugendstil, leaving its false start at a second nature in order to take up this new compositional approach using geometric and proportional construction, it was as if the Nietzschean vitalism of his crystalline designs for the Darmstadt artists' colony had settled into the calmness of the grid, now confident in its capacity, as a generalizable schema, to generate a new self-reflexive order for the entire built environment, from furniture to buildings to site plans. Projects such as his Düsseldorf Garden Exhibition 1904, were understood to deploy geometry not in the Platonic sense of pure forms, but as a neo-Kantian architectonic, a logical geometrical matrix that regulated and coordinated the formation (*Gestaltung*) of objects in space and time.[45] Like Ernst Cassirer and Erwin Panofsky's later formulations of the idea of symbolic form[46] or Conrad Fiedler's earlier formalist conception of language,[47] these matrices of generative design practices may be understood as early efforts to develop, model, and theorize architectonics as a system of mediation between subject and object — at once natural and human. Eisenman's own relentless experimentation with theories and models of that interface has been explicitly critical of metaphysical claims such as Lauwericks might have made. Yet, something of the neo-Kantian, post-metaphysical striving to theorize the conditions of possibility of knowledge remains, albeit framed in terms of social, cultural, and technological constructs as much as logical, mathematical, or architectonic ones. Eisenman's Max Reinhardt Haus may be understood, then, as part of an ongoing work on models of mediation, a project not unlike that of an inventor striving for the perfect machine, which, like a submarine, would carry us through the dark and murky depths to reach firm ground at the bottom of the sea. As one prototype after another fails to achieve this goal, their accumulation becomes testimony to the impossibility, and necessity, of such experimentation.[48]

In his reworking of Kant, the early nineteenth-century philosopher Arthur Schopenhauer used the phenomenon of crystallization as an example of will, which he understood precisely as *not* representation, but rather as "the being-in-itself of every thing in the world." While the crystal was, for him, a low form of objectification — bone formation was higher — it marked "a perfectly definite and precisely determined striving in different directions constrained and held firm by coagulation"[49] and as such could exemplify the conflict between force and matter, will and representation that Schopenhauer saw throughout nature. While nature, he explained, only exists through this conflict, it engenders competition among phenomena striving to appear, each snatching the matter from one another in order to reveal its own Idea. Thus, when crystals "in the process of formation meet, cross, and disturb one another ... they are unable to show the purely crystalline form."[50]

The fearsome and alienating effect of Eisenman's seemingly deformed, if not deranged, Max Reinhard Haus — in his own words, a "blasphemous object" — is the result of the mutual deformation of two generative structures competing for matter — the partial and modified Möbius strip colliding "insanely" with the conventional building type of the high-rise tower or, more specifically, the familiar suburban model of twin towers on a podium. Where the double structures of Eisenman's early houses lent themselves to an interpretation by Rosalind Krauss as "hermeneutic phantoms"[51] — the second and functionally redundant structure deployed to re-present the other in the self-reflexive loop of a formalism unconcerned to see beyond itself — the Max Reinhard Haus compounds structures that are radically at odds with each other. This doubling produces an uncanny estrangement from the normative conceptions of architecture by materializing the violence of exclusion endemic to all structurings. Is it the office building that struggles to be released from the grip of the Möbius strip, or is it the Möbius strip that so desperately longs to be recognized within the conventional twin towers? In either event, the objective of refounding architecture rationally and essentially in its own architectonics — in formal structures, geometries, and technologies understood to operationalize the Kantian a priori category of space — has been scrambled. Each structure interferes with the other's quest for authority, bringing that quest itself into visibility. Just as overlaying two similar patterns produces a moiré effect, so Eisenman's doubling of generative matrices produces an unfamiliar and uncomfortable zone beyond them, crystallized into an unprecedented object.

The Suprematist Kazimir Malevich, too, was interested in how change occurs in the body of art. Based on the proposition that "the activity of the painter is a combined function of the conscious and subconscious [or supraconscious] mind," he argued in his treatise on the nonobjective world that a change in the world (outside art) introduces a new "additional element" into the conscious system of art through the subconscious "creative organism" of the artist. The artist thereby destroys existing norms and produces new forms by causing existing ones to evolve or by overthrowing them.[52] While life, Malevich contended, strives for a state of rest, inactivity, and the "natural" by setting up norms and systems that transform dynamic elements into static ones, "every construction is dynamic because it is 'on the way' toward a system." So it is that the early public perception of Cubism as "abnormal" and "unwholesome" was, according to Malevich, a consequence of the antagonism of two coexistent artistic norms — one naturalistic, the other pictorial. While Malevich's well-known response was to eliminate "things" in favor of pure art, feeling, and abstraction, the political implications of attempting to implement such purifying utopias have resulted in a loss of innocence over the course of this century, giving new value to those impure and unwholesome experiments that aim to change "things" by introducing new "additional elements." Produced in transit, Eisenman's "thing" marks the fluidity of closure for architecture itself, the liminal threshold of the crystalline architectonic matrix.

Farshid Moussavi and Alejandro Zaera-Polo's project for the Yokohama International Port Terminal (construction to commence 1997) also operationalizes the process of crystallization in time, not however through formal transformations, but by registering the life of the building itself. Submerged below the surface of objecthood, the terminal's roof extends the space of the city into the waterfront as a constantly shifting ground for unprogrammed public activities. The building strives to avoid the mediations of representational systems and seeks instead the character of a living "artifact," its folded steel-plate topography changing continually as a fluid index of the ebb and flow of crowds moving within, from cruise ships to land and back again. Although this fluctuating membrane displays the direct pulse of inner life, the immediacy of this expression is overtly technological, and the gesture becomes rhetorically self-reflexive as the surface assumes the character of an object after all; suspended above the water, its dependence on subsurface forces is made visible from the harbor. Understandable once again within the quest for a second nature that incorporates the human and non-human, construction here is no longer thematized in terms of the fixed contours of elemental purity, but becomes a dynamic and open surface responsive to invisible shaping forces whose objectification in turn offers a platform for the unforeseen.

Fig. 8. Le Corbusier, Villa Savoye, Poissy, 1928–31: view from the landing of the second floor looking toward the ramp and terrace. Reproduced from Willy Boesiger, Le Corbusier and Pierre Jeanneret: Oeuvre complète de 1929-34 (Zurich: Les Éditions d'Architecture [Artemis] , 1964), p. 27.

Time

Just as the proposal for a Sea Terminal for the Belgian coast (competition 1989) by Rem Koolhaas and Office for Metropolitan Architecture aimed to be fully artistic and fully efficient at the same time — a frictionless unity of art and technology — so it folds together other seemingly opposed categories (open-closed, abstract-figural, machine-body, opaque-transparent, whole-fragmented). Eliding the recognizable, it sets in motion a machine for producing endless trains of associations — mechanical, industrial, utilitarian, abstract, poetic, surrealist — and delirious combinations of spatial experiences orchestrated in time. Part nihilistic sphere for a transient and uprooted modernity (Ledoux) and part elementarized head for a mechanical-organic humanity (Oskar Schlemmer), the transit station rises from the point of contact between ground and sea, receiving its guests submerged, entombed, and contained. Yet, no sooner have they arrived than the structure spins them into a disoriented orbit, which serves to reorient them within the landscape of the building and the landscapes beyond. In its upper reaches, opportunities to reenact the stasis of everyday life are augmented by the seductions of hovering and groundless distractions, releasing the polymorphous potential of the body's contours under the cranium of the galaxy.

Recalling the much smaller but similarly eroded volume, docking system, ramps, private rooms, viewing platforms, and pleasure zones of Le Corbusier's Villa Savoye (1928–30), the temporary domicile of the Sea Terminal suggests reconsidering Sigfried Giedion's notoriously elusive concept of space-time. "It is impossible," wrote Giedion in his 1941 Space, Time and Architecture, "to comprehend the Savoye house by a view from a single point; quite literally, it is a construction in space-time. The body of the house has been hollowed out in every direction: from above and below, within and without. A cross section at any point shows inner and outer space penetrating each other inextricably."[53] As Giedion observed, this experience is "latent in the skeleton system of construction, but the skeleton had to be used as Le Corbusier uses it: in the service of a new conception of space. That is what he means when he defines architecture as *construction spirituelle*" (fig. 8). If transparency was Giedion's aim, and clearly he found it in the Villa Savoye, it was certainly not a transparency of substance, as Colin Rowe and Robert Slutzky later presumed,[54] but rather the transparency of subject and object mutually constructing and mediating each other, characterized by Giedion in the language of dissolution, metamorphosis, and interpenetration. He referred to Le Corbusier's poetics as transmuting the raw material of construction and approaching the problem of the house with a "seismographic delicacy" of perception, "freeing it from its inherited ponderousness" by incorporating "the floating counterbalance of forces, the lightness and openness, which nineteenth-century iron construction succeeded in expressing in abstract terms." Considered in this way, transparency marks neither pure invisibility nor pure visibility, but rather the mediation whereby immateriality surfaces through material bodies and substance floats in the unstable flux of materialization, dematerialization, and rematerialization.

Key to Giedion's poetic and phenomenological conception of architecture in the modern symbolic form of space-time was the notion of *Gestaltung*, understood not only in terms of production, but in terms of reception as well. For like van Doesburg and Moholy-Nagy,[55] Giedion considered the viewer to be an active participant in the formation of buildings and spaces. As he made clear in his depiction of the Bauhaus at Dessau, the building cannot be comprehended, its gestalt cannot be known, until the observer has experienced the building all around, inside and out. Its identity as object, necessarily contingent on experience, is inevitably incomplete, limited to the cumulative acquisition of partial perspectives and movements of perception across time. As Franz Roh had suggested of Post-Expressionism, here the thing must be constantly formed anew, its static form merely the coordinate of the fourth dimension.

If this seems a long way from Le Corbusier's insistence on the plastic effect of mass referred to earlier, it may be worth recalling that his position had in fact changed by the mid-1920s in both his painting and architecture. Attuned to these changes, Giedion's reading of the Villa Savoye in 1941, like his earlier reading of the housing estate at Pessac (1924–26), points to the link between these architectural works and the second generation of Purist painting, exemplified by the *Still Life* (fig. 9) that Le Corbusier had featured over the dining table in his Pavilion Esprit Nouveau (1925). Where earlier Purist paintings were distinguished by the compression and layering of purified opaque objects into a two-dimensional spatiality, the later works slide out from under the rigor of linear, architectonic objectivism into the aqueous, perhaps even oceanic, space of humor that Robert Slutzky has so eloquently described.[56] (Giedion noted that Jeanneret and Ozenfant had themselves developed the idea of the *mariage des contours* in relation to these paintings and suggested that the space-time properties of Pessac and Savoye marked the transposition of this effect into architectural form.[57]) In the later Purist paintings, morphology and structure (compositional and spatial) become mutually conditioning as volumes are simultaneously asserted and denied, flattened, compressed, and rendered transparent. By these means, space becomes a thor-

Fig. 9. Charles-Edouard Jeanneret, Still Life for Pavillon de l'Esprit Nouveau, 1924. Oil on canvas, 12 1/2 x 15 3/8 in. Courtesy Fondation Le Corbusier, Paris.

oughly ambiguous condition within a transparent tapestry of oscillating contours and contrasts, plans and elevations, foregrounds and backgrounds. The eye and its spatial imagination are invited to move freely, rather than objectively, within this diaphanous and porous structure, its vibrations dislodging the binary categories of gestalt psychology into something approaching the constitutive ambiguity of phenomenology. While these paintings signal a departure from Purism's initial rejection of Cubism and a certain revisiting of its architectonic, they neither explode nor deform objects in order to inscribe the participation of the observer, but rather conserve their normative constitution while opening these objects up to contingency within a spatial matrix. This matrix not only holds and delineates objects in relation to each other, but is itself constituted in the perception of those relations. It does not exist objectively in space, but is instead an effect that resides in the event and temporality of observation, in the interface between subject and object.

Giedion's description of the equivalent effect in Le Corbusier's architecture at Pessac invokes the experiences of an observer in motion appreciating, through parallax, the phenomenon of "corners merging into one another," of clear independent volumes collapsing into two-dimensionality only to spring back into depth a few steps later.[58] The importance assigned by Giedion to this effect is revealed in the less guarded and almost ecstatic prose of the earlier book, where he defends the paperlike thinness of the buildings — their solid volumes eaten away with cubes of air, rows of windows passing suddenly into the sky — because they "create ... as in a snowy landscape in the right light . . . that dematerialization of the firmly demarcated which renders upward and downward slopes indistinguishable and makes the walker feel as though he is striding through clouds."[59] Similarly, his description of the Villa Savoye continually implies an observer experiencing the interpenetration of inner and outer space through framed views of the landscape, moving up and down, and in and out along the ramp. While Le Corbusier's fascination with perception in motion is well-known,[60] what remains less so is the explicitness with which he linked his notion of the architectural promenade to this perceptual game. In the commentary that accompanies the La Roche-Jeanneret Houses of 1923 in the *Oeuvre complète*, he describes the experience of the promenade not only as a spectacle of perspectives developing with great variety but also as an essay in polychromy that engenders a "camouflage architectural" in which volumes are both "affirmed and effaced."[61] This double and contradictory moment — assertion and denial, positive and negative, form and formlessness — is also the key property of the marriage of contours, exploiting the properties of transparent objects such as bottles to be both themselves and not themselves at the same time, autonomous and self-estranging, closed and open to beyond. Through the techniques of camouflage, which he had previously disparaged in *Après le cubisme* (1918), the painter-architect began to create the effects of his paintings in architecture.

In the sphere of painting, Jeanneret generated oscillation as a movement exclusively in the eye, on an axis with the retina, in keeping with a conception of vision as fundamentally two-dimensional and of depth as an effect generated by layered planes — a theory put forward by the sculptor Adolf Hildebrand in a highly influential treatise of 1893.[62] But rather than aiming for the truest representation of objects in space, as Hildebrand and his colleague the proto-Purist painter Hans von Marèes had done, the marriage of contours partially dissolved the object into a relational network, a kind of liquid space in which objects and spatial rela-

Fig. 10. Theo van Doesburg and Cornelius van Eesteren, Maison Particulière, 1923: axonometric projection. Ink, gouache, and collage, 22 1/2 x 22 1/2 in. Van Eesteren-Fluck & van Lobuizenstichting, Amsterdam. Photo: Nederlands Documentatiecentrum voor de Bouwkunst.

tionships became mutually mediating in perception over time, no longer locked into a binary movement between figure and ground, foreground and background, but now free to move in a less determined way — more lateral, dynamic and open-ended.

In architecture, Le Corbusier first ventured to transpose this play of contradictions into the housing at Pessac, painting the concrete walls in colors that dissolve their mass into surface. Here and in the later villas, he recognized that the medium of architecture differs from painting in that the movement of the observer takes place in psychophysiological rather than purely optical space. Le Corbusier's deployment of color in this way, as well as his transposition from painting into architecture, is entirely consistent with the work of van Doesburg and Cornelius van Eesteren undertaken for the De Stijl exhibition at Léonce Rosenberg's Paris gallery in 1923 — a show that is known to have impressed Le Corbusier while finalizing his La Roche-Jeanneret Houses. Here, van Doesburg demonstrated his recent breakthrough in experimenting with color on buildings, something he had begun in collaboration with J.J.P. Oud in 1917–18 and which he considered to be an extension of, and correction to, the elementarism of analytical Cubism as well as Apollinaire's programmatic reception of it as inaugurating a new reality. Working in 1923, van Doesburg discovered that by coloring the surfaces of an axonometric drawing by van Eesteren for the Rosenberg Houses (fig. 10), the closed mass of the building could be elementarized and opened up in space-time, transforming cubic blocks into crystalline structures of two-dimensional surfaces.[63] The uncolored counter-reliefs of transparent planes that van Doesburg then abstracted from the building were taken by Giedion as exemplary of the modern space conception, a kind of ideal image for which the houses remained contingent manifestations, still marked by a contradiction between closed and open structures not unlike the double structure that Malevich had so disdained in Cubism's figural abstractions. Yet, it is this stalled state of materialization — of matter failing to leave itself behind in the quest for idealist spatial experience — this obdurate insistence of the body on the impossibility of purity as well as the necessity of purification, this sustained contradiction of the object in and of the space of perception, that now matters in the context of monolithic architecture.

Although Giedion and the Purist Le Corbusier may be understood as aiming for the transcendence of matter, which Giedion called the poetics of space-time and Le Corbusier called ineffable space, they considered this pursuit as necessarily mediated by bodies and their palpable complicity with the fluid field of spatial forces within which experience is constructed. Just as the marriage of contours in Le Corbusier's Villa Savoye, as in his paintings, served to configure the complicity of the object with the space of observers and producers — as that complicity was understood then — so Koolhaas's project for Zeebrugge provides a representation of it which extends the phenomenology of perception to incorporate the technological mediation of perception. Where, following the lead of Hegel and the art historian Alois Riegl, Moholy-Nagy imagined history as an inexorable progression from the massive, solid, archaic blocks of the Egyptian pyramids to the ephemeral dematerializations of layered grids, open spatial fields, and light architecture (fig. 11), Koolhaas's station bends the line of history upon itself, bringing its two ends into contact.

Fig. 11. Two images from László Moholy-Nagy's Von Material zu Architektur (1928), depicting the Pyramid of Mykerinos (ca. 3250 BC) as the beginning of what Moholy-Nagy took to be the development of architectural history: from the solid, monumental Block to the dematerialized, interpenetrating spatiality of modern Architecture. The latter is exemplified by Jan Kamman's double-exposure double-portrait of the Van Nelle Factory in Rotterdam (Brinkman and van der Vlugt, architects). Reproduced from László Moholy-Nagy, Von Material zu Architektur (Mainz: Florian Kupferberg, 1968), pp. 97, 236.

Autonomy

To reconsider the status of architectural objects, recognizing that, like identities and bodies, objects are continuing to be constructed, would require an understanding of how these constructions are contingent on the complex apparatus that regulates their production and audiences — on geometries and technologies that construct, on social conventions and institutions that structure, on professions and bureaucracies that regulate, and on economies and cultures that flow. And it would have to accept the task of theorizing, visualizing, or otherwise modeling this ultimately unrepresentable matrix, constituted, like language, only through repeated performance. But because the coordinating grid is more accurately not a thing but a set of practices performed again and again, it can be changed. By rethinking the self-reflexivity of architecture's autonomy as the self-reflexivity of the matrix of practices that defines architecture, it may be possible to think autonomy together with its critiques, to move from a discourse of autonomous form, which sees its task as assimilating new work to an already given body of forms, to one that provides knowledge of those norms sufficient to open them to new possibilities, to potentialities beyond norm and form.

The projects in this exhibition represent local, partial, and exceptional transformations of the regulatory matrix, which if generalized would engender greater tolerance for what the Italian philosopher Gianni Vattimo has described as the tendency of our time — of new media and the global redistribution of power — to weaken the principle of reality.[64] Such tolerance asks for the confident and creative acceptance of the impossibility today of a single monolithic construction of "the real" and fuels the ongoing, necessary, and amazing process of passionately dematerializing and rematerializing realities as fiction, art, and dreams, knowing that we (individually and collectively) are dreaming.

Recent theories and practices within the contemporary architectural avantgarde have privileged fragmentation, instability, uncertainty, and fluidity to generate formal worlds that could be understood as sublime, formless, or beyond representation, in the hope that these would make room for alterity, abjection, and marginality. The notion of monolithic architecture, provoked by projects of these same architects, may be seen to rework this aim more "realistically" and within the constraints of the architectural object — its given economies, cultures, materialities, and promises of security. Rather than presuming to be able to step outside the matrix of normative practices, these works accept their inexorable complicity with it, yet strive like "insider critics" to transform it as they reiterate its scripts.[65]

The extraordinary buildings that comprise monolithic architecture take up aspects of ordinary buildings produced so routinely by the regulatory matrix as to constitute a kind of collective automatic writing: they assume the formal rigors of simple, economical structures with tight enclosing envelopes, sufficiently charged to generate a recognizable and consumable image and installed seamlessly into the grid of metropolitan infrastructure and the landscapes of suburban and ex-urban development. Within this grid of generative factors, the simple containers of monolithic architecture introduce the unexpected and estranging, the magical and mysterious, the shocking and seductive, the dreamy and fantastical, the terrifying and austere. Constitutive instabilities within the matrix are exploited using quintessentially architectural techniques: working the abstract contours of building enclosures into ambiguous figural identities; exaggerating size and scale to produce effects of presence that exceed the objective limits of the object; using colors, materials, finishes, and profiles to strategically invest the surfaces that mediate between the inside and the outside with qualities that demonstrably overflow the boundaries of conventional architecture; and shaping interior experiences into complexities that range from darkness to splendor to transcendence. By cutting, folding, twisting, and corroding the closed surfaces of the monolith, it becomes simultaneously open, radiant, and resonant; by giving its skin the elasticity to respond to internal pressures, external processes, and the flow of time, it assumes a complexity and a dynamic that exceed the common notion of identity, that understand it in terms of contingent effects that can no longer be taken as identical with the objects that they name. Estranging and self-alienating, these effects depend on the relation between subject and object, on perception in time and motion, and on the capacity of the cognitive faculties to circumscribe their own limits *and* remain attuned to potentialities beyond those limits — in a word, on the ability to hold autonomy and alterity together in a single image. All this within building types that Robert Venturi, in the 1960s, might have called dumb and ordinary.

Of course, the disdain of Venturi and his colleagues for the abstract yet metaphorically charged "duck" buildings of modernists such as Paul Rudolphe could extend to these shaped and figured monoliths.[66] Yet, Venturi's interest in complexity and contradiction, and even the populist realism attributed to him by Jorge Silvetti as a conscious concern for the representation of reality,[67] could equally be attributed to monolithic architecture, despite its refusal to engage in the semiotic play of ornament and icon which remains Venturi's calling card. Monolithic architecture too enjoys the mimetic impulse, not, however, as limited to the hermetic games of liberties and supplementarities structured within systems of representation, but through critical and poetic transformations that play against those systems, imagining them in other ways and inhabited by other subjects. Where Venturi's mimetic practices — especially his distortions and hybridizations — politely loosened the conventions of verisimilitude to include the popular and vernacular, the mimesis of monolithic architecture is more radical and addresses the claims of modern architecture to crystalize other realities. If an opera house can, in Philippe Starck's words, recall "the whale that swallowed Mecca," if its huge dimensions can give it "the weight of a black hole," and if it can, seemingly by itself, metamorphose into a "non-building" (with the same space efficiencies and cost per square foot as a gilded palace), then the understanding of architecture as normative has been expanded, not just a little, but almost beyond grasping. Or, more precisely, almost beyond the grasp of that semiotic language into which humanity's ancient capacity "to become and behave like something else" has passed during two millenia of Western rationality, as the critic Walter Benjamin pointed out in the 1930s.

While Benjamin distrusted archaicisms, he nevertheless wrote of the continued importance of the mimetic faculty as humanity's capacity to play at self-estrangement, at being other. Yet, this capacity to produce and read magical correspondences in sensuous things, so familiar to ancient people, had, he contended, passed in the modern era entirely into the nonsensuous realm of language. Benjamin welcomed this, for it seemed to liquidate the power of magic, which he feared had become, like archaicism, all too easily drafted into the service of regressive phantasmagoria and myth. For Benjamin, the mimetic faculty could now only manifest itself, like a flame, through a kind of bearer, which he took to be the semiotic dimension of language: "Thus the coherence of words or sentences is the bearer through which, like a flash, similarity appears. For its production by humanity — like its perception by it — is in many cases, and particularly in the most important, limited to flashes. It flits past."[68] But what of architecture, whose sensousness had led Hegel to position it as the lowest medium of expression while elevating philosophy — the nonsensuousness of language — to the top? And what of these monolithic architectures, as heavy as black holes and as light as crystals, their mimetic capacity borne by the semiotic technologies that regulate the contemporary production and reception of buildings? Are their effects not also limited to flashes of recognition? Do they not likewise merely flit past in the momentary perception of observers drawn into the orbit of collapsing dualities?

1 Jean Nouvel, "The Crucible", in *Jean Nouvel, La Obra Reciente 1987–1990/ His Recent Works 1987–1990* (Barcelona: Quaderns Monografies, 1990), p. 64.

2 Franco Bertoni, *The Architecture of Philippe Starck* (London: Academy Editions, 1994), p. 76.

3 Karl Scheffler, *Moderne Baukunst* (Leipzig: Julius Zeitler, 1908), p. 12.

4 Alfred Gotthold Meyer, *Eisenbauten: Ihre Geschichte und Aesthetik* (Esslingen: Paul Neff Verlag, 1907).

5 Ibid., pp. 11, 64, 78, 148.

6 Michael Fried, "Art and Objecthood" (1967; reprint in Gregory Battcock, ed., *Minimal Art: A Critical Anthology* [New York: E.P. Dutton, 1968], pp. 116–47). The critical discourse associated with the essay includes the exchange between Fried, Rosalind E. Krauss, and Benjamin H.D. Buchloh, "Theories of Art after Minimalism and Pop," in Hal Foster, ed., *Discussions in Contemporary Culture* (Seattle: Bay Press, 1987), pp. 55–87, as well as Rosalind E. Krauss, *Passages in Modern Sculpture* (Cambridge, MA: MIT Press, 1977), chaps. 6–7; and T.J. Clark, "Clement Greenberg's Theory of Art"; Michael Fried, "How Modernism Works: A Response to T.J.Clark"; T.J.Clark, "Arguments about Modernism: A Reply to Michael Fried," in Francis Frascina, ed., *Pollock and After: The Critical Debate* (New York: Harper and Row, 1985), pp. 47–88.

7 Fried, "Art and Objecthood" (note 6), pp. 117–18. Clement Greenberg introduced the notion of literalness to distinguish post-Cubist sculpture from the conception of traditional sculpture in his essay "The New Sculpture" (1949; reprint in John O'Brian, ed., *Clement Greenberg: The Collected Essays and Criticism*, vol. 2 [Chicago: University of Chicago Press, 1986], pp. 313–19).

8 See "Questions to Stella and Judd," interview by Bruce Glaser, ed. Lucy R. Lippard, *Art News* 65 (September 1966), pp. 55–61.

9 Clement Greenberg, "Modernist Painting" (1961; reprint in John O'Brian, ed., *Clement Greenberg: The Collected Essays and Criticism*, vol. 4 [Chicago: University of Chicago Press, 1993], pp. 85–93.

10 Fried singled out the work of Anthony Caro and David Smith. See, for instance, Clement Greenberg, "Sculpture in Our Time" *Arts Magazine* (1958; reprinted in *Clement Greenberg* [note 9], pp. 55–61). Greenberg's critique of Minimalism is found in "Recentness of Sculpture" (1967; reprint in *Clement Greenberg* [note 9], pp. 250–56).

11 Fried, "Art and Objecthood" (note 6), pp. 137–38.

12 See Yve-Alain Bois, "Kahnweiler's Lesson," *Painting as Model* (Cambridge, MA: MIT Press, 1990), pp. 65–97.

13 See Robert Morris, "Notes on Sculpture, Part 2" (1966; reprint in Robert Morris, *Continuous Project Altered Daily: The Writings of Robert Morris* [Cambridge, MA: MIT Press, 1993], pp. 11–21).

14 Fried, "Art and Objecthood" (note 6), p. 138.

15 The empathists included Wassily Kandinsky and August Endell; Conrad Fiedler and Adolf Hildebrand developed the formalist conception of corporeal knowledge, also on empathetic and psychophysiological bases, but emphasizing cognition rather than feelings. Fried made his debt to Merleau-Ponty's philosophy of the body explicit in *Discussions in Contemporary Culture* (note 6), p. 72.

16 Fried, "Art and Objecthood" (note 6), pp. 146–147.

17 See Krauss (note 6), chaps. 6–7; Rosalind Krauss, "Overcoming the Limits of Matter: On Revising Minimalism," in *American Art of the 1960s*, exh. cat. (New York: Museum of Modern Art, 1991), pp. 123–141.

18 Quotations are from *American Art of the 1960s* (note 17), pp. 138–39.

19 Rosalind Krauss, "The /Cloud/," in Barbara Haskell, *Agnes Martin*, exh. cat. (New York: Whitney Museum of American Art, 1992), pp. 155–65; idem, "Cindy Sherman: Untitled," *Cindy Sherman 1975–1993* (New York: Rizzoli, 1993).

20 *American Art of the 1960s* (note 17), pp. 128–29.

21 See Kenneth E. Silver, *Esprit de Corps: The Art of the Parisian Avant-Garde and the First World War, 1914–1925* (Princeton: Princeton University Press, 1989); Elizabeth Cowling and Jennifer Mundy, *On Classical Ground. Picasso, Léger, de Chirico and the New Classicism 1910–1930*, exh. cat. (London: Tate Gallery, 1990).

22 Amédée Ozenfant and Charles-Edouard Jeanneret, *Après le cubisme* (Paris: Edition des Commentaires, 1918), p. 58.

23 Le Corbusier, *Towards a New Architecture* (London: Architectural Press, 1974), p. 28.

24 Ibid., p. 31.

25 Ibid., p. 37.

26 Ibid., p. 39.

27 For an interpretation of Behrens's work as exemplary of the "new Renaissance" in its pursuit of a neo-Kantian conception of form, see Julius Meier-Graefe, "Peter Behrens," *Dekorative Kunst* 8, no. 10 (July 1905), pp. 381–90.

28 This is made explicit in the concluding lines of Emil Kaufmann, *Architecture in the Age of Reason: Baroque and Post-Baroque in England, Italy, France* (Cambridge, MA: Harvard University Press, 1955).

29 Hans Sedlmayr, *Verlust der Mitte* (Salzburg: Otto Müller Verlag, 1948) (Eng. trans. by Brian Battershaw as *Art in Crisis: The Lost Centre* [London: Hollis and Carter, 1957]).

30 Ludwig Hilberseimer, *Großstadtarchitektur* (Stuttgart: Julius Hoffmann, 1927), pp. 99–100.

31 Ludwig Hilberseimer, *Contemporary Architecture: Its Roots and Trends* (Chicago: Paul Theobald and Company, 1964), pp. 104–31.

32 Ibid., p. 104.

33 See Walter Benjamin, "Erfahrung und Armut, 1933," *Gesammelte Schriften*, vol. 1, pt. 1 (Frankfurt a/M: Suhrkamp, 1991), pp 213–19; Heinrich Zille, *"Mein Milljöh": Neue Bilder aus dem Berliner Leben* (Hannover: Fackelträger, 1977).

34 Franz Roh, *Nachexpressionismus: Magischer Realismus: Probleme der neuesten europäischen Malerei* (Leipzig: Klinkhardt und Biermann, 1925).

35 Franz Roh, *German Art in the Twentieth Century: Painting, Sculpture, Architecture* (London: Thames and Hudson, 1968), pp. 112–14.

36 See also Wieland Schmied, "Neue Sachlichkeit and the German Realism of the Twenties," in *Neue Sachlichkeit and the German Realism of the Twenties*, exh. cat. (London: Hayward Gallery, 1978), p. 9.

37 Roh, *Nachexpressionismus* (note 34), pp. 53–57.

38 Roh, *German Art* (note 35), pp. 137–38.

39 See David E. Wellbury, *Lessing's Laocoon: Semiotics and Aesthetics in the Age of Reason* (Cambridge: Cambridge University Press, 1984).

40 Sigfried Giedion, *Bauen in Frankreich: Eisen, Eisenbeton* (Leipzig and Berlin: Klinkhardt und Biermann, 1928).

41 Sigfried Giedion, *Space, Time and Architecture* (Cambridge, MA: Harvard University Press, 1941), pp. 19–20.

42 See "Women + Technology: An Interview with Sadie Plant by Lachlan Brown," *Work* 1 (1994), pp. 12–18.

43 B.J. Novitski, "Freedom of Form," *Architecture*, no. 8 (August 1994), p. 107.

44 J.L.M. Lauwericks, "Einen Beitrag zum Entwerfen auf systematischer Grundlage in der Architektur," *Ring*, no. 4 (1904), pp. 24–35. See also Von Cees Zoon, "Auf dem Wege zu einer monumentalen 'Nieuwe Kunst' — Die Proportionslehre und Entwurfstheorie von J.L. Mathieu Lauweriks," in *Maßsystem und Raumkunst: Das Werk des Architekten Pädagogen und Raumgestalters J.L.M. Lauwericks*, exh. cat. (Krefeld: Kaiser Wilhelm Museum, 1988), pp. 33–54.

45 See Meier-Graefe (note 27).

46 Erwin Panofsky, *Perspective as Symbolic Form*, trans. Christopher S. Wood (New York: Zone Books, 1991); Ernst Cassirer, *The Philosophy of Symbolic Forms* (New Haven: Yale University Press, 1955).

47 For Fiedler, "the relation betwe3eech, but identical with it." See Conrad Fiedler, "Erkenntnis Theorie" and "Bemerkungen über Wesen und Geschichte der Baukunst, *Schriften zur Kunst* (Munich: Wilhelm Fink, 1971), vol. 2, pp. 62–94, 429–80.

48 I am grateful to Kurt Forster for this striking image.

49 Arthur Schopenhauer, *The World as Will and Representation* (1818), vol. 1, trans. E.F.J. Payne (New York: Dover, 1969), p. 118.

50 Ibid., pp. 147–49.

51 Rosalind Krauss, "Death of a Hermeneutic Phantom: Materialization of the Sign in the Work of Peter Eisenman," *Architecture + Urbanism* 112 (January 1980), pp. 189–219.

52 Kasimir Malevich, *The Non-Objective World*, trans. Howard Dearnstyn (Chicago: Paul Theobald and Company, 1959), pp. 12–14.

53 Giedion (note 41), p. 416.

54 Colin Rowe and Robert Slutzky, "Transparency: Literal and Phenomenal," *Perspecta* 8 (1963), pp. 45–54.

55 See Theo van Doesburg, *Grundbegriffe der neuen gestaltenden Kunst* (Frankfurt a/M: Oehms, 1925); László Moholy-Nagy, *Von Material zu Architektur* (Munich: Albert Langer, 1928) (Eng. trans. by Daphne M. Hoffman and enlarged as *The New Vision* [New York: George Wittenborn, 1947]).

56 Robert Slutzky, "Acqueous Humor," *Oppositions* 19–20 (Winter–Spring 1980), pp. 29–51.

57 The idea of the marriage of contours was introduced by Jeanneret and Ozenfant in "Idées personnelles," which appeared in *L'Esprit nouveau*, no. 27 (November 1924), and again in *La Peinture moderne* (1925). Their discussion is accompanied not only by plates of paintings but also by diagrams showing the compositional structure of two paintings, one by Ozenfant, the other by Jeanneret.

58 Yve-Alain Bois has discussed the play of parallax in architecture and in the art of Richard Serra, defining parallax, from the Greek *parallaxis*, as "change" and "displacement of the apparent position of a body, due to a change of position of the observer." See Yve-Alain Bois, "A Picturesque Stroll around *Clara-Clara*," *October* 29 (1984), pp. 32–62.

59 Giedion (note 40), p. 85.

60 See, for instance, Le Corbusier's statement that it is "by walking, through movement, that one sees an architectural order develop" (*Oeuvre complète de 1929–1934* [Zurich: Editions d'Architecture, 1964], p. 24). Bois has linked Le Corbusier's promenade, specifically that of the Villa Savoye, to the parallax effects in the work of Richard Serra; see Bois (note 58).

61 W. Boesiger and O. Stonorov, *Le Corbusier et Pierre Jeanneret: Oeuvre complète 1910–1929* (Zurich: Editions d'Architecture, 1964), p. 60.

62 Adolf Hildebrand, "The Problem of Form in the Fine Arts," in Harry Francis Mallgrave and Eleftherios Ikonomou, eds., *Empathy, Form, and Space* (Santa Monica: Getty Center for the History of Art and the Humanities, 1994), pp. 227–79.

63 See Yve-Alain Bois, "The De Stijl Idea," *Painting as Model* (Cambridge, MA: MIT Press), pp.101–22.

64 Gianno Vattimo, *The Transparent Society*, trans. David Webb (Baltimore: Johns Hopkins University Press, 1992).

65 Arguments for this kind of transformative criticism have been developed in gender studies and critical legal studies; see Judith Butler, *Bodies That Matter: On the Discursive Limits of "Sex"* (New York: Routledge, 1993); Diana Fuss, *Essentially Speaking: Feminism, Nature and Difference* (New York: Routledge, 1989); Drucilla Cornell, *Transformations: Recollective Imagination and Sexual Difference* (New York: Routledge, 1993). I owe the term "insider critics" to Brian Boigon; see also "Insider Criticism: Sandra Buckley, Manuel De Landa, Bruce Ferguson and Bruce Grenville," in Brian Boigon, ed., *Culture Lab* (New York: Princeton Architectural Press, 1993), pp. 17–58.

66 Robert Venturi, Denise Scott Brown, and Steven Izenour, *Learning from Las Vegas* (Cambridge, MA: MIT Press, 1972), esp. "Explicit and Implicit Associations," pp. 92–93.

67 Jorge Silvetti, "On Realism in Architecture," *Harvard Architectural Review* 1 (Spring 1980), pp. 11–32. Silvetti pointed to the effects of estrangement achieved in different ways by the distortion of the real in the work of Aldo Rossi as well as Venturi.

68 Walter Benjamin, "The Mimetic Faculty," in Peter Demetz, ed.; Edmund Jephcott, trans., *Reflections* (New York: Harcourt, Brace, Janovich, 1978), p. 335.

Wilfried Wang

In Search of Aura

> When we come across a mound in the woods, six feet long and three feet wide, raised to a pyramidal form by means of a spade, we become serious and something in us says: somebody lies buried here. *This is architecture.*[1]

The current collective phenomenon of buildings that appear as if they were monolithic, as if they were made of a single piece of stone, may have at least two fundamental roots. The first could be said to relate to architecture's communicative role, while the second might be argued to stem from architecture's historical development. Though recognizing that these two roots may even intertwine, that their separate discussion is to some extent artificial and indeed probably part of the assumption that has led to the belief in the relevance of buildings as monoliths, for the purpose of this essay, the bifurcation will be applied to clarify this search for aura in architecture, a search that will be argued to be closely connected with the occurrence of buildings as monoliths.

In this essay, a building as monolith is considered as a structure whose apparent communicative presence strikes us by its singularity in form and possibly also by its sheer size. It may be rather simple in its configurations, whose regularity we may grasp immediately, whose outward appearance seems to guarantee its inner constitution — indeed, whose representative might is founded on its material and, by idealized implication, on its conceptual integrity.

The appearance of a number of monolithic buildings in recent years should be seen in the broader context of contemporary practice. In its multiplicity of forms, symbols, and gestures, architecture of the late twentieth century has revealed a richness and diversity hitherto neither consciously nor willingly registered by orthodox architectural historians. This contextual diversity extends beyond the matter of form; it certainly includes ideological and philosophical issues. The appearance of monolithic buildings may thus be regarded as a reaction to this conscious awareness not merely of contemporary diversities but also of those of the past, a reaction that betrays itself when this diversity is referred to in terms of "disorder" or "chaos."

Some architects may at times argue that the proclivity for more or less compact forms is intimately tied to constructional processes, inherent programs, prevailing site and climatic conditions. These variables, however, cannot be argued to determine form entirely. Deep-rooted proclivities for more or less compact forms are also dependent on architects' belief in the communicative role of buildings. There are architects who maintain that built forms can and must communicate, and others who are less confident in this belief. There are even those who hold that, in a multimedia culture, architecture can or should only mediate without

recourse to symbolic or iconographic form, that it should employ elements immanent to its discipline, that mediation is possible only through nonfigurative, abstract ambience. At the extreme ends of the subdivision, then, there are architects who contend that buildings communicate through symbols, who regard signs as active emitters of meaning, and those who consider that buildings and their various parts create more or less distinct compositions, whose expressive values might well be understood without recourse to a complex set of external references. It is within this broad spectrum of beliefs that the phenomenon of buildings as monoliths is to be discussed.

This essay will not deal with the extensive etymology of the term *aura*. Suffice it to state that the search for aura in architecture is itself part of the remythologization of both processes of signification and making in architecture. The roots as well as the concept of aura are part of a distant, golden era, whose authoritative structures enshrined values in cult objects without the possibility of doubt in terms of those values' rationality or durability. Both these aspects were often reinforced, so to speak, by the objects' pragmatic facticity, which lent them their expressive radiance. The paradigm for such an apparent unity has often been argued to mark both the beginning of architecture and the end of human life: it is burial structures that indistinguishably unite authoritative legitimation of values and material instantiation in monolithic objects. And it was this apparently self-originating force of the object that led such architects as Adolf Loos to assert where they believed that the "true" locus of architecture was to be found.

Architecture, Communication, and Precedent

> Architecture arouses sentiments in man. The architect's task therefore is to make those sentiments more precise. The room has to be comfortable; the house has to look habitable. The law courts must appear as a threatening gesture towards secret vice. The bank must declare: here your money is secure and well looked after by honest people.
> The architect can only achieve this if he establishes a relationship with those buildings which have hitherto created these sentiments in man . . .
> Our culture is based on the all-surpassing grandeur of classical antiquity. We have adopted the technique of thinking and feeling from the Romans.[2]

Over numerous centuries, this kind of observation of a built edifice — a manner of reading which presupposes an existing "vocabulary" — has had to contend with the rise and development of other media, whose ability to bear more specific information with less inaccurate transmission of the contained ideas has increasingly cast architecture aside. This gradual eclipse of architecture as a medium for the communication of ideas, and therefore as a domain of knowledge which both controls and processes a range of ideas, has been witnessed with different degrees of consciousness by the architectural profession. Architectural practice, theory, and modes of representation, the fields of activity under the more or less direct auspices of architects, have seen developments that have sought to clarify and strengthen the significance of built edifices.

Acknowledging the rise and increased number of other media, as well as their relatively more accessible codes, some attempts in architecture have sought to overcome the seeming complexity and opacity of architecture's iconography by presupposing the existence of irreducible and essential forms of universal significance.[3] As mentioned earlier, one of the loci of this discussion can be found in the subject of burial structures or tombs. The menhir, the dolmen, the pyramid, and, more specifically, the mausoleum are precedents on which self-evident communication is argued to be based. It is this notion of self-evidence — the obviousness of a form, its ability to project meaning without apparent recourse to a pre-existing vocabulary or references — that could be argued to lie at the heart of architecture's attempt at retrieving that radiance which great edifices of the past were said to have possessed, that wordless mediation of an easily understood idea, that golden silence with which a building, so to speak, glows; in short, that aura surrounding past cult objects.

History: The Search for Aura in Architecture

> Ultimately, the general, preeminent characteristic of Greek masterpieces is a noble simplicity and a calm grandeur . . .[4]

It would not be the first time that contemporaneous developments, whether in architecture or in other cultural domains, have been viewed in relation to history. The seeming authority of precedent, of the past — especially a venerated one — has been invoked by most architects who have published their thoughts. Such historical contexts, even such distant periods as those of ancient Athens or Rome, have served to set selected aspects of what have been assumed by writers to be universally admired paradigms of good taste against problematic aspects of their contemporaneous developments. Such paradigms were to be valued, studied, copied, or reproduced. Combined with this process of eclectic legitimation, architectural theory, or at least writing that may be regarded as having some theoretical content, has also sought to unravel some of the more mysterious variables of its discipline, variables that are at the heart of architecture's ability to mediate intention, meaning, and character. Precedents would be read in an abstract way; a schema, for example, composed of a range of basic geometric forms, would be superimposed to suit the argument. Such discussions have tended to follow an analytical route, seeking to relate specific forms to specific meanings and characters. If these two dimensions of the architectural discourse are systematically traced over the past two and a half centuries, their remarkable constancy — the clear separation of historical development from more abstract, theoretical considerations (together with the evident inability of the historical dimension to be reconciled with autonomous morphological analyses) and the stridency of the orthodox view — set the backdrop for successive calls to and from the concentrated architectural statement, the simply recognizable form, the authoritative object: the monolith.

The constancy of the historical and analytical dimensions and the stridency of the orthodox view should be seen against other interpretations of architecture's potential development. The density of an object of aesthetic contemplation, its value or character, has been the subject of theoretical considerations. Different views of how character could be mediated in formal compositions emerged, for example, from the eighteenth-century debates in aesthetics and landscape theory. For instance, whereas Edmund Burke defined "beautiful" forms as simple, smooth, and uniform in surface,[5] Uvedale Price maintained that beauty solely defined in Burke's terms was inadequate and that compositions that were "interesting to the cultivated eye"[6] contained a mixture of beautiful and picturesque moments, the latter consisting of "two opposite qualities of roughness and of sudden variation, joined to that of irregularity."[7] The picturesque embodied the romantic spirit, its love of mature landscapes, old oak trees, ruins of temples, contrasting light and shade, marks of time as in patina-encrusted buildings. The picturesque admitted transience as a category of contemplation, it embraced the concept of accretion and decay, of growth and the organic, and in so doing foreshadowed the arguments of the subsequent two centuries.

A building's intimate relation with its users and its contexts, climate and culture, would render it a receptacle of forces that would initially, even at the design stage, and ultimately leave their marks on it. The reception of an ideal intention on a built form as well as the built form itself, acting as an extension to everyday life, frame the range of interpretations of the organic in architecture. From Gottfried Semper and Eugène Viollet-le-Duc to Hugo Häring and Sigfried Giedion's belated lament, architects and critics have sought to put the generally alternative case for designing architecture not by predetermining form, but by identifying the building's inherent particularity.[8]

Both strategies recur today: formal concentration as well as the urge to transcend the significance of form or, at least, to attempt to dissolve its visual hegemony of "strong" and "weak" form. From the vantage point of the organic thesis, the return of the "monolith" may be interpreted as seeking to purge the excesses in the cynical exploitation of debased architectural motifs (usually classicizing ones), while simultaneously reasserting the authority of the architectural discipline (perhaps also that of the particular commissioning client) and, by extension in the case of public commissions, maybe even that of conventional social stratification.

Fig. 1. Adolf Loos, Max Dvořák's Tomb. Reproduced from Ludwig Münz and Gustav Künstler, Der Architekt Adolf Loos (Vienna: Anton Schroll, 1964), p. 189.

Thus, for example, superficially reminiscent of Neoclassicism's displacement of the apparently playful late excrescences of the Baroque — of the Rococo[9] — it might be argued that the recurrent use of geometrically concentrated forms sought the establishment of different ideological orders. Here, we might be reminded of Etienne-Louis Boullée's series of cenotaph projects (as, for instance, the cenotaph to Newton [1784; fig. 2]), whereby the inconsequential fritterings of late eighteenth-century society were condemned, to be replaced by the resurrected heroes of the Enlightenment. Or we might even recall some examples from Russian Constructivism, wherein we might read the sweeping away of late nineteenth-century Russian society; in this context, we might cite Ivan Leonidov's project for the Lenin Institute (1927; fig. 3).[10] Indeed, the case might be made that in both these instances, the reuse of regular, geometric, quasimonolithic forms could be regarded as an attempt to symbolically surmount previous social structures. Undoubtedly, architects such as Boullée or Leonidov were convinced of architecture's capacity for such symbolic determinism, of the power to symbolically replace despotic regimes by visually striking and formally intense architectures. However, the contemporary reuse of monolithic forms cannot be regarded as being founded on the same belief in symbolic determinism as its predecessors. Seeing these monolithic forms in present differentiated practice, they do not share the revolutionary zeal of a Boullée or a Leonidov project. If anything, today's monolithic forms are restorative, seeking to replace the fragmentation, the formal diffusion, the incomprehensibility of theoretically supported complexities, and the abstraction of the last three decades by objects that contend with internal mat-

Fig. 2. Etienne-Louis Boullée, Cenotaph to Newton, 1784: elevation. Reproduced from Jean-Marie Pérouse de Montclos, Étienne-Louis Boullée (Paris: Flammarion, 1994), p. 153.

ters: the reestablishment of architecture's authority, the plea for its autonomy, and, by extension, the status of the client, the architect, and the discipline as a whole.

Extending this argument on the reuse of monolithic form to the question of whether such forms reaffirm social structures in flux does not seem credible from the current perspective. Despite the increased significance of many other media to the detriment of architecture, the latter's power of formal determinism remains unique, even if sensibilities for precise observation of architectural phenomena have been waning for some time. Profane architecture as the handmaiden to secular ideologies still takes the physical place of religion; its aesthetic experience by contemporary society is still able to compete with currently revitalized mystical revelation. The reuse of monolithic forms may thus be understood in the general context of competing mediating disciplines, of rival forms of knowledge, to which architecture, with its occasional claim to autonomy, has long sought to belong. The current reuse of the monolithic in architecture may thus be argued to seek, above all, the restoration of a wordless radiance, of the auratic moment previously the privileged domain of cult objects. It is in this sense that we may understand the footnote in Walter Benjamin's essay "The Work of Art in the Age of Its Technical Reproducibility":

> The definition of aura as a "unique phenomenon of a distance, however close it may be" represents nothing other than the formulation of a cult value of the work of art in categories of space-time perception. Distance is the obverse of closeness. The essential quality of distance is unapproachability. Unapproachability is indeed a major quality of the cult image. True to its nature, it remains "distant, however close it may be." The closeness which one may gain from its subject matter does not impair the distance which it retains in its appearance.[11]

A corollary to this quality of unapproachability is that of unknowability, achieved through the silent and homogeneous shrouding of the singular form. As such, the monolithic form defies questioning; it presents a mysterious exterior. The respective material realizations of this shrouding indicate the degree of mystery sought: smooth stone without pronounced joints suggests a gravelike muteness; faceted sheets of tinted glass with matching silicone joints increase our curiosity, tantalizing us with a seeming transparency, yet leaving only fragmented reflections.

The Belief in Aura and Its Dialectic in Architectural Practice

To most architects and architectural critics, buildings continue to be considered as elements in a process of communication. Buildings are thought to mediate values and ideas by their formal appearance. Their overall form, their configuration or massing, are assigned certain meanings; they are each thought to have more or less specific significance. From the most concentrated form — the building as a symbol — to the most diffuse agglomeration of pieces, each building, it is thought, can be viewed and conceptually questioned in terms of its supposed meaning:

> You employ stone, wood and concrete, and with these materials you build houses and palaces. That is construction. Ingenuity is at work.
> But suddenly you touched my heart, you do me good, I am happy and I say:

"This is beautiful." That is Architecture. Art enters in.

My house is practical. I thank you, as I might thank Railway engineers, or the Telephone service. You have not touched my heart.

But suppose that walls rise towards heaven in such a way that I am moved. I perceive your intentions. Your mood has been gentle, brutal, charming or noble. The stones you have erected tell me so. You fix me to the place and my eyes regard it. They behold something which expresses a thought. A thought which reveals itself without word or sound, but solely by means of shapes which stand in a certain relation to one another. These shapes are such that they are clearly revealed in light. The relationships between them have not necessarily any reference to what is practical or descriptive. They are a mathematical creation of your mind. They are the language of Architecture. By the use of raw materials and *starting from* conditions more or less utilitarian, you have established certain relationships which have aroused my emotions. This is Architecture.[12]

As distinct from Loos (see his 1913 essay "Architecture"), Le Corbusier suggested in this passage that meaning could be established without words, description, without context and history. It was Le Corbusier and Amédée Ozenfant who, in modern times, argued for the conceptual imperative, in which forms are the "mathematical creation of the mind" (1923). In *Vers une architecture* (Toward a new architecture), this sentiment is well defined:

A clear aim, the classification of parts, these are a proof of a special turn of mind: strategy, legislation. Architecture is susceptible to these aims, and repays them with interest. The light plays on pure forms, and repays them with interest. Simple masses develop immense surfaces which display themselves with a characteristic variety according as it is a question of cupolas, vaulting, cylinders, rectangular prisms or pyramids. The adornment of the surfaces is of the same geometrical order. The Pantheon, the Colosseum, the Aqueducts, the Pyramid of Cestius, the Triumphal Arches, the Basilica of Constantine, the Baths of Caracalla.

Absence of verbosity, good arrangement, single idea, daring and unity in construction, the use of elementary shapes. A sane morality.[13]

In *Après le cubisme* (After cubism; 1918), Ozenfant and the then Charles-Eduard Jeanneret had put the case for a return to the "invariant":

Purism does not express variations, but rather the invariant. The work is not to be accidental, exceptional, impressionist, inorganic, contestatory, picturesque. On the contrary, it is general and static; it expresses the invariant.

Purism wants to conceive clearly, execute loyally, precisely, without any waste; it turns away from muddled conceptions, expedient and rough executions. A serious art should banish any technique that deters from the real value of the conception.[14]

The invariant was the historically constant, the theoretically permanent, the geometrically recognizable, the mathematical creation of the mind, the ideal of Purism. Reference to ancient Rome was not made by accident; the well-known sketch from *Vers une architecture* became the reductive extract from this interpretative analysis (fig. 4). These geometric objects, it was suggested, have inherent, autonomous meaning. The reference to ancient Rome metonymically and elliptically established an autonomous meaning with a seemingly independent authority. The geometric bodies of cylinder, pyramid, cube, stele, and sphere exude authority through their very solidity. They were considered to emit exact messages

They were thought to radiate meaning through their very ideal, irreducible form — that is, through their geometrical essence. Disassociating meaning from historical context, ambiguously disconnecting references from specific instances while still referring to real cases, rescuing, or at least attempting to rescue, architectural form in its geometric purity for a new and paradoxically invariant language prepared the path for pure and compact forms, so as to speak, with an inner authority.

The grounds that were laid by the Purists lacked real foundations. There was the implication that meaning could exist without context or precedent, with geometry being conceived of as possessing dimensions it never had: points have no size, lines no thickness, planes no depth, volumes no material presence. Believing, then, that Purist architecture could simply rely on rendered surfaces, painted white and other Purist colors, introduced a profound contradiction in a desired, renewed *architecture parlante*: its authority shorn of any physical reality, reduced to unaccountable, invisible substructures, decorated with plaster that was not detailed to show any age, resisting patina and other excrescences.

Thus, the momentous debate, which included the enquiry into the role of ornament[15] and its gradual excision from orthodox modern architecture, the autonomization and reification of functions as determinants of architectural form, and the implications of individual hygiene and social pathology — in short, the disappearance of the authority of form through the instrumentalization of architecture — simultaneously induced a compensatory, and at times desperate, belief in monolithic form.

When Otto Wagner suggested that "the panel-like treatment of surfaces, the greatest simplicity, and an energetic emphasis on construction and material will thoroughly dominate the newly emerging art-form of the future,"[16] he was accurately predicting the course of modern architecture with the exception of the energetic emphasis on construction and material. These aspects too would gradually disappear in view of the increased autonomization and specialization of constructional processes and elements. Ever thinner and lighter materials, ever quicker processes — as again foreshadowed by Wagner, though with a somewhat naïve optimism — have rendered both construction and material mute, save for the outermost surface. Thus, layers upon layers remain the last constructional syntax of architecture: the greatest simplicity resides in the panel-like treatment of surfaces. This is essence implied and thus projected, clarity of image and purity of form by default. The compensatory and desperate belief in architecture's semantic radiance was of necessity simultaneous to this gradual process in the phenomenal reduction of architecture's real gestation and presence. But rather than consciously redefining Wagner's prediction for contemporary conditions, the underlying nostalgia for a consistent, systematic, linear logic, wherein each component of a building is to reverberate in harmony with an originating concept, should be openly discussed in order to avoid a futile effort at redefinition. While such a nostalgia for consistency is undeniably present in much architectural thinking, it is necessary to recall that, just as contemporary constructional technology undermines such a longing for conceptual integrity, so too are formal desires for compact shapes contradicted not only by prevalent detailing standards but also by the theoretical roots on which the desire for monolithic architecture has been based.

Fig. 3. Ivan Leonidov, Lenin Institute, 1927. Reproduced from Ivan Leonidov, <u>Ivan Leonidov</u> (New York: Rizzoli, 1981), p. 37.

Order and Authority, Aura and Autonomy

In the historical context, buildings tending toward the monolithic might be regarded as emerging in contradistinction to the seemingly decadent diversity of contemporaneous architecture with the purpose of re-establishing a sense of outward calm and order. Such a renewed *rappel à l'ordre*[17] would seek to rally the faithful to architecture's defence. Thus, the search for aura in architecture can also be related to the desire to maintain its intellectual and cultural independence, an independence that could be considered as architecture's claim to the profane belief in transcendence, its hope to inherit the cult value of eclipsed religion.

In so far as this is indeed sought by architecture, the logical consequence has been pursued. The belief in the importance of the visual sense, thereby the importance given to the form, the object, is paramount. The building as monolith to be beheld assumes the quality of a totem. As a totem, a building exudes authority. However, it is the physical independence of the object that necessarily returns to reinforce the error in the belief in the existence of architecture's absolute autonomy. A separate object, especially a building as monolith, suggests closure and self-containment, its authority underlined by its constructional detailing: occasional seamless connections, large and repetitive cladding elements, uniform materials belying the complexity of the actual construction. Hollowness, as previously alluded to, is of greater destructive force to the authority of a building than any other syntactical error. Discovering that a stone facade consists merely of slabs hung off metal brackets from a steel subframe by accidentally knocking at its surface; noticing that a prefabricated plaster panel has come undone in the ceiling to reveal a void filled with ducts and cables; or sensing that a carpet-covered aluminum floor panel rests on adjustable metal feet, and that only the carpet pattern guarantees the seeming continuity of the floor surface — all these experiences literally and conceptually undermine any effort at restoring authority to the discipline via the creation of buildings that hope to reclaim special significance through their concentrated form.

In giving the visual sense preeminence, architectural effort and debate have been dominated by formal issues. This reliance on the visual to create the "real" world results in icons of solidity redoubling the sense of disappointment on witnessing the true hollowness of clad monolithic forms, a contradiction that is immanent to the logic of an architectural image no longer able to fulfil the constructional reality of its imagined material cohesion. Creating seemingly monolithic buildings and searching for aura in architecture may be a valiant enterprise, just as are many other pursuits of contemporary architecture. It is, however, also a futile exercise as long as it fails to grasp the numerous logical contradictions.

True authority may only be restored to the architectural discipline when it realizes that its sensory dimensions are not solely restricted to the visual realm, that the environment is experienced through a combination of senses, including the haptic one, which requires no scholarly iconographic knowledge. An architecture that consciously appeals to a combination of senses might then be able to transcend the recurrent discussion about figuration or abstraction, including the fixation on powerful forms such as seeming monoliths, and focus on space and its syntax. The aura that was hitherto thought to radiate from forms might then once again be intuited in the amazement of spaces.

Certainty in an age of change, authority in the context of ideological diversity, monolithic building as a restoration of certainty and authority, are strategies

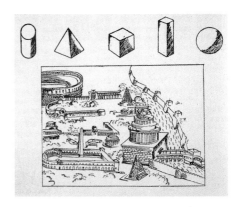

Fig. 4. Le Corbusier, sketch of Ancient Rome with geometric solids. Reproduced from Le Corbusier, <u>Vers une architecture</u> (Paris: Editions Vincent, Fréal & Co., 1958), p. 128.

with immanent dialectic. Whether meaning can really be ascertained through such strategies has been discussed in this essay. In transcending the once closed unity of the Pyramids, reaching the developed diversity of nineteenth-century historicism, it is possible not to return simply to a closed unity of architectural forms, but to a diverse unity of true cultivation,[18] in which the visual sensibility is but part of a range of sensibilities, and therefore no longer in a position to dictate concepts for perceiving and designing architecture. Before this stage of an architectural culture is reached, however, the close identification of the designing ego with the object needs to be considerably relaxed. Otherwise, the immanent logic of architectural theory and formal compositions will continue in its ever more desperate search for the relevance of a meaningful architecture wherein meaning is reduced to a building's outward appearance.

Such a desperate search will reveal nothing other than a faint echo like the sound emitted by a cladding panel struck in error, itself like the rays of a melancholic afterglow from the mythic era once redolent with aura.

1 Adolf Loos, "Architecture"(1913), in Yehuda Safran and W. Wang, eds., *The Architecture of Adolf Loos* (London: Arts Council of Great Britain, 1985), p. 108.

2 Ibid.

3 See Dagobert Frey, *Grundlegung zu einer vergleichenden Kunstwissenschaft* (Vienna: Rohrer Verlag, 1949). Frey's comparative analysis of cult edifices throughout the world posits the existence of two basic configurational devices: processional and static "motives."

4 Johann Joachim Winckelmann, *Gedanken über die Nachahmung der griechischen Werke in der Malerei und Bilhauerkunst* (1756; Stuttgart: Reclam, 1969), p. 20 (English translation by the author).

5 Edmund Burke, *A Philosophical Enquiry into the Origins of Our Ideas of the Sublime and Beautiful* (1757; Menston: Oxford University Press, 1970), sec. XIV, p. 103–4.

6 Uvedale Price, *An Essay on the Picturesque, as Compared with the Sublime and the Beautiful; and, on the Use of Studying Pictures, for the Purpose of Improving Real Landscape* (London: J. Robson, 1794), p. 87.

7 Ibid., pp. 46–47.

8 Gottfried Semper, "Entwerf eines Systems der vergleichenden Stillehre," in Hans and Manfred Semper, eds., *Kleine Schriften* (Mittenwald: Maander, 1979), pp. 259–91.

9 Eugène-Emanuel Viollet-le-Duc, "Style," *Dictionnaire de l'architecture française au XVe et XVIe siècles* (Paris, 1866), vol. 8, p. 476; Hugo Häring, "Wege zur Form," in Heinrich Lauterbach and Jürgen Joedicke, eds., *Hugo Häring* (Stuttgart: Karl Krämer Verlag, 1965), pp.

13–14; Sigfried Giedion, *Mechanization Takes Command* (New York: Oxford University Press, 1948), pp. 714–723.

9 Hugh Honour, " . . . art begins to replace religion and the aesthetic experience the mystical revelation. . . ," *Neo-Classicism* (London: Pelican, 1968), p. 60.

10 For a complete thesis on the similarity and differences between so-called revolutionary architectures, see Adolf Max Vogt, *Russische und französische Revolutionsarchitektur 1917–1789* (Cologne: Dumont, 1974).

11 Walter Benjamin, "Das Kunstwerk im Zeitalter seiner technischen Reproduzierbarkeit," trans. in *Illuminations* (London: Fontana, 1973), p. 245.

12 Le Corbusier, *Towards a New Architecture* (1923), trans. F. Etchells (London: Architectural Press, 1946), p. 141.

13 Ibid., pp. 146–47.

14 Amedée Ozenfant and Charles-Eduard Jeanneret, *Après le cubisme* (Paris: Edition des Commentaires, 1918), pp. 59–60.

15 See Otto Wagner, "Style," *Moderne Architektur* (Vienna, 1896), or Adolf Loos, "Ornament and Crime" (1913), in *The Architecture of Adolf Loos* (note 1), pp. 100–03.

16 Otto Wagner, *Moderne Architektur*, 4th edn. (Vienna, 1914), p. 136 (Eng. trans. in *Modern Architecture* [Santa Monica: Getty Center for the History of Art and the Humanities, 1988], p. 125.

17 Jean Cocteau, *Le Rappel à l'ordre* (1923) (Eng. trans. New York: Haskell House, 1974), pp. 123–25, 176–80.

18 Georg Simmel, "Der Begriff und die Tragödie der Kultur," *Das individuelle Gesetz* (Frankfurt/M: Suhrkamp, 1987), p. 118.

Spiro N. Pollalis

Computed Monoliths

Computer-aided architectural design has begun to have an impact on the production of architecture. Although the main focus has been on the automation of laborious drafting, new uses are emerging beyond the development of construction drawings. Computer-based modeling provides a rich medium for conceptual design explorations, and direct links to manufacturing allow the implementation of complex architectural designs with more accuracy and less detailed documentation on paper. Seen as another medium for carrying out a design, computing should have the same impact on monolithic architecture as on the design of any other type of building. However, monolithic architecture places a special value on a building's *concept*. As if made from a single piece of stone carved from within, a monolithic structure requires a certain cohesiveness that originates from a single idea and that is carried out by selecting consistent construction materials and details, with emphasis on the complex elements that comprise the building's skin.

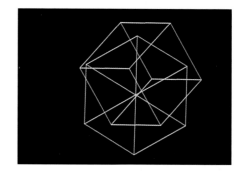

Fig. 1. William J. Mitchell, 1990: computer model of design concepts based on geometric operations on a solid. Courtesy William J. Mitchell.

The computing environment is quite powerful in allowing a single designer to be in charge from conception through construction, especially during certain stages of the design process. These are:

- the creative stage of conceptual design;
- simulations on the computer model;
- the development of construction drawings; and
- the fabrication of parts of buildings.

Among the projects discussed in this volume, Peter Eisenman's Max Reinhardt Haus, Philippe Samyn's Walloon Forestry Department Shell, and Farshid Moussavi and Alejandro Zaera-Polo's Yokohama International Port Terminal are examples of buildings in which computing was employed in the design process.

The Creative Stage of Conceptual Design

The use of computing in the creative stage of conceptual design is still in development.[1] It is already clear that operations on simple geometric objects can lead to complex design solutions (fig. 1).[2] Such operations can apply to creating the exterior shape of a building, as well as to defining interior space or building components.

In the design of the Max Reinhardt Haus, Eisenman followed such a technique of operating on geometric objects (fig. 2). The entire conceptual design was carried out on the computer, in a constant dialogue between the designer and the machine. With very few sketches and no architectural drawings at all, Eisenman

discussed his concept of the Möbius strip with the computer operator, who modeled it on the computer. The focus then became the materialization of a crystalline structure. Different alternatives were visualized and studied with computer models. During those studies, a series of variations of the parameters defining the Möbius strip were tested.

The interior space of Eisenman's building was also studied on the computer. A cube traveling along the Möbius strip defined this interior space, with varying heights of one, two, or three cubes, depending on the function of each of its parts. Various relationships were studied between the Möbius strip and the movement of the cube, using a software package that produces plots of mathematical functions. Those functions explored the visual effects of several such relationships, such as the cube following a path perpendicular to the surface of the strip, or a path inclined to the surface of the strip. The preferred design scheme was produced by the cube moving in such a way that its major diagonal was always coplanar to the surface of the strip. Subsequently, the computer model was modified to fit on a structural grid. In the end, the computer model generated the components to make an actual three-dimensional model. The data was exported to a laser cutter that cut the Plexiglas pieces of the facade, and those pieces were then assembled by hand. While construction drawings have not been produced for this project, the geometric computer model provides the basis for them.

Although there was no programming involved in the design of the Max Reinhardt Haus other than defining the functions in the mathematics software, the analytical geometrical operations enhanced a creative use of computers in conceptual design. Recently, the programming of discrete steps of the creative process has also been explored. George Liaropoulos has automated the theoretical searches for House X, as described by Eisenman, and has demonstrated the potential of the computer medium not only to provide the framework for graphics manipulation but also to prescribe certain manipulations that can be carried out quickly and precisely.[3]

Moussavi and Zaera-Polo also chose the computer as the appropriate design environment for the Yokohama International Port Terminal. After a few sketches on paper, they drew the sections along the pier to fulfill the program requirements. Then, through morphing, they generated the geometry of the structure (fig. 3). According to Zaera-Polo, "[T]he computer became an inseparable part of the process of design." The computer model helped in the visualization of the building and allowed the designers to make modifications and use the model as a means for team communication. Interestingly, the designers themselves worked on the computer in the early stages of the conceptual design, without the mediation of computer operators. After the form of the building had been determined, a team of operators developed the detailed architectural drawings for the project. In those drawings, the computer environment helped the architects to take into consideration the manufacturing and construction constraints involved in forming the complex double-curved surfaces. As Zaera-Polo noted, "the computer changes the premise on which designers work, and redefines the way we think the design of buildings."[4]

Fig. 2. Peter Eisenmann, Max Reinhardt Haus, 1992: computer rendering. Courtesy Eisenman Architects.

Fig. 3. Farshid Moussavi and Alejandro Zaera-Polo. Yokohama International Port Terminal, 1995: axonometric drawing of a series of sections. Courtesy Foreign Office Architects.

Simulations on the Computer Model

A geometric model on a computer can do more than simply provide a graphic representation of the building-to-be. It can provide information on the behavior of that building and serve as a testing ground for alternative design schemes and for selecting appropriate construction materials. This is how Philippe Samyn used a computer to design the Walloon Forestry Department Shell.

The commitment of Samyn's firm to engineering and computer technology was inspired by Samyn himself, who studied engineering prior to architecture. As he has explained, his approach to designing a building concentrates on three parts: geometry, materials, and the environmental behavior of the building, or "building physics," as it is called in Europe.[5] The latter constitutes studies of lighting — both daylight and artificial light — interior climate, interior air flow and variations of temperature, and acoustics. The firm's commitment to computing extends from making geometric models to studying "building physics" in order to obtain optimal spaces.

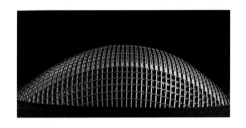

Fig. 4. Philippe Samyn, Walloon Forestry Department Shell, 1995: rendering of computer model. Courtesy Samyn and Partners.

The conceptual design for the Walloon Forestry Department Shell was carried out on paper in the form of sketches and drawings that defined the basic geometry of the building. This allowed for quick changes and design investigations. When the basic geometry had been defined, a three-dimensional geometric model was developed on the computer (fig. 4). That model helped to visualize the geometry and to transfer the necessary information for structural analysis for determining the sizes of the structural members. Paying attention to constructability, the model was modified so that the whole structure could be fabricated out of eight different sizes of wooden members with rectangular sections, all approximately 20 feet in length.

Samyn, however, considers that the real thrust of computing in the Walloon Forestry Department Shell came from the steps that followed. The computer model was used to study the building's environmental behavior in detail. The building's shape made it a candidate for the greenhouse effect, so the first studies concentrated on selecting the right glass panes. Different panes were considered in terms of shading effect, heat transfer, and heating and cooling requirements, as well as reflective capacity. Those studies suggested that laminated polyethylene glass with the outer sheet coated with metal oxides would be the best choice, from both architectural and technical points of view. The slightly reflective glass was modeled on the computer to behave reflectively or transparently, depending on the time of the day. The choice of single glass panes increased the need for climate control inside the building. Spot heating was considered in order to save energy, and the computer model showed that it would be a wise solution. Interior air ducts shaped like bananas suck up warm air in summer, while in winter warm-air boosters help to create a more uniform climate.

The Development of Construction Drawings

Today, design firms use computers mostly for generating construction drawings. The construction drawings for Samyn's Walloon Forestry Department Shell were produced using computer-aided drafting (fig. 5). The detailed three-dimensional model provided the exact geometry of the building by specifying the coordinates of every single point and by defining the sections of the three-dimensional object with the planes of the drawings. The advantages of using the computer to develop the construction drawings were easy to quantify. The drawings had the same complexity as other construction drawings produced by the office, and they were produced in record time. In addition to saving time on the drafting board, the drawings were so exact that they provided the 18 different contractors with a reliable base for developing shop drawings and for producing the treated wooden members.

Although the development of construction drawings on the computer is quite common practice, the drawing of the Walloon Forestry Department Shell in this manner was particularly important as it did not have any repetitive plans. Unlike an office building or housing complex, segments of whose plans recur, the Walloon Forestry Department Shell has a unique geometry and details. Thus, the computer was used to focus on describing a single, unique object. In a similar manner, the three-dimensional computer models of Eisenman's Max Reinhardt Haus and Moussavi and Zaera-Polo's Yokohama International Port Terminal will serve as the basis for developing construction drawings in the future.

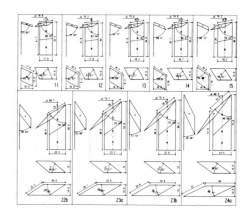

Fig. 5. Philippe Samyn, Walloon Forestry Department Shell, 1995: construction detail. Courtesy Samyn and Partners.

The Fabrication of Parts of Buildings

Initially, computers were used in architectural firms as substitutes to carry out the same tasks that had been accomplished by human beings. In the late 1980s, computer advocates became more aggressive, proposing to "re-engineer" any process that had been designed before information technology had become available.[6] Important questions arose regarding the "re-engineering" of design and construction drawings. With computers available to store, retrieve, and process information throughout the stages of design and construction, architects were able to take over responsibilities that had fallen to subcontractors and other professionals in earlier times. The firm of Frank Gehry was among the first to make changes in the way the design process was handled, using computers to develop complex shapes on screen and sending this information directly to fabricators. Gehry's office started producing the equivalent of shop drawings, thus assuming design responsibility well beyond that usually taken by offices.

Unlike Gehry, Samyn did not attempt to make a direct link between the design and the automated fabrication of the components of the Walloon Forestry Department Shell. Recognizing that the contractors were small and that the Belgian government wanted to keep construction local, he did produce shop drawings with exact dimensions. Thus, the builders were able to make the formwork for the concrete elements and cut the treated wooden members of the structure using traditional methods with accuracy and efficiency. In the case of the Yokohama International Port Terminal, Kawasaki Steel has already produced a mock-up of the double-curved surface that will make up the roof of the building, using computer-based manufacturing techniques and data from the computer model provided by the architects. All parties agree that the making of the roof forms would not be feasible from an economic point of view without computer-aided manufacturing, and they expect that the construction of the building will rely heavily on computer use.

While computer models and animations based on those models can be powerful tools with which designers can present their ideas to clients, none of the projects featured in this catalogue — or any other notable examples of monolithic architecture — have been presented in computer models to patrons as a means of convincing them about the validity of the projects. The three computer-dependent projects in this exhibition employed computing as a design tool rather than as a simple representation method. Can computing then be said to enhance monolithic architecture? Clearly, the real push from computing in architecture consists in lowering the barriers to innovative design. Computing can facilitate the development of projects allowing the testing of complex design alternatives and by providing more specific parameters regarding the implementation process and construction details, thus making innovative projects buildable.

1 See Spiro N. Pollalis, "Towards the Automation of Conceptual Design," in A. Tzonis and I. White, eds., *Automation Based Creative Design: Current Issues in Computers and Architecture* (Amsterdam: Elsevier, 1994).
2 See William J. Mitchell, "A New Agenda for Computer-Aided Design," in M. McCullough, W.J. Mitchell, and P. Purcell, *The Electronic Design Studio: Architectural Knowledge and Media in the Computer Era* (Cambridge, MA: MIT Press, 1990).

3 See George Liaropoulos, *Programming for Making the Drawings for House X*, private archive, New York, 1995.
4 Alejandro Zaera-Polo, telephone interview by author, May 1995.
5. Philippe Samyn, telephone interview by author, May 1995.
6 See Hammer Michael, "Re-engineering Work: Don't Automate, Obliterate," *Harvard Business Review* , no. 4 (July-August 1990).

THE PROJECTS

PETER EISENMAN
Eisenman Architects
The Max Reinhardt Haus

JACQUES HERZOG AND PIERRE DE MEURON
Herzog & de Meuron
Signal Box auf dem Wolf

REM KOOLHAAS
Office for Metropolitan Architecture
Sea Terminal

RAFAEL MONEO
José Rafael Moneo, Architect
Kursaal Cultural Center and Auditorium

FARSHID MOUSSAVI AND ALEJANDRO ZAERA-POLO
Foreign Office Architects
Yokohama International Port Terminal

JEAN NOUVEL
Jean Nouvel and Associates
The New National Theater

PHILIPPE SAMYN
Samyn and Partners
Walloon Forestry Department Shell

PHILIPPE STARCK
Starck
The Baron Vert

SIMON UNGERS AND TOM KINSLOW
Simon Ungers, Architect
T-House

PETER EISENMAN

Eisenman Architects

The Max Reinhardt Haus

Berlin, Germany

Designed: 1992

The site for Peter Eisenman's unbuilt Max Reinhardt Haus occupies a position on the north bank of the Spree River in the vicinity of a railroad station and near the intersection of the two major cross-axes in Berlin, Unter den Linden, running east–west, and Friedrichstrasse, oriented north–south. The proximity to these traffic arteries signals the location's status as an important juncture for the city. Major development projects in the surrounding areas and the historic significance of the district promise a revival to this area. Eisenman's 34-story, multi-use tower commemorates a figure in the district's history, the well-known theater owner Max Reinhardt. Reinhardt's Schauspielhaus once stood on the site, which now plays host to a number of theatrical establishments.

Aiming to engage a diverse public, Eisenman's tower contains a hotel and related conference facilities, a health club, a media center, and a vertical mall, as well as offices and restaurants. A portion of the complex houses the Max Reinhardt Forum, comprising the Max Reinhardt Archiv, a flexible theater, and facilities devoted to promoting the history of theater and film. The deliberately high concentration and variation of commercial, consumer, and experiential possibilities mirror the density of function in the metropolitan surrounds. In addition to its recreational character, the building appears as a singular presence on the Berlin skyline.

Beginning with the concept of the Möbius strip — a two-dimensional entity with a single, continuous surface that twists in on itself — Eisenman arrived at the series of topological surfaces through a process of mathematical manipulation and computer projection. Each two-dimensional plane was then connected to the others, generating the building's "folded" volumes. The entire design process relied on — and was made viable by — computer modeling technology, which enabled the production of complex volumes and irregular geometries. The resulting prismatic form, according to Eisenman, acquired "the capacity to represent on one site that which is of many places . . . gathering the diffuse and unstable bits and pieces of the city into a kaleidoscopic array." Not only did the Max Reinhardt Haus evolve from the particularities or conditions of its geological, urban, and historical sites; it also folds in upon itself the contextual implications of the surrounding environment without hierarchic bias or predisposition. The enormous, multifaceted structure undergoes a constant play of light, shadow, and reflection across its crystalline glass surfaces and metallic edges, thus engendering links between the site and the metropolis at large.

The prominent posture of the building establishes it as a conspicuous landmark in keeping with earlier proposals for this district, including one by Mies van der Rohe for his first skyscraper. Eisenman's building assumes a symbolic role in the city as a landmark that becomes integral to the collective urban experience. Its twisting form commands a visual presence projecting well beyond the bounds of the tower's immediate surroundings. As such, the Max Reinhardt Haus fulfills the need for a symbolic gateway to Berlin, functioning as a metaphorical anchor for the larger initiatives to develop the nearby districts and fashioning a recognizable identity for Berlin as a world city.

Note

The quotation from Peter Eisenman was taken from a project text provided by the architect.

1 Presentation model.

2

2 Section b.
3 South elevation.

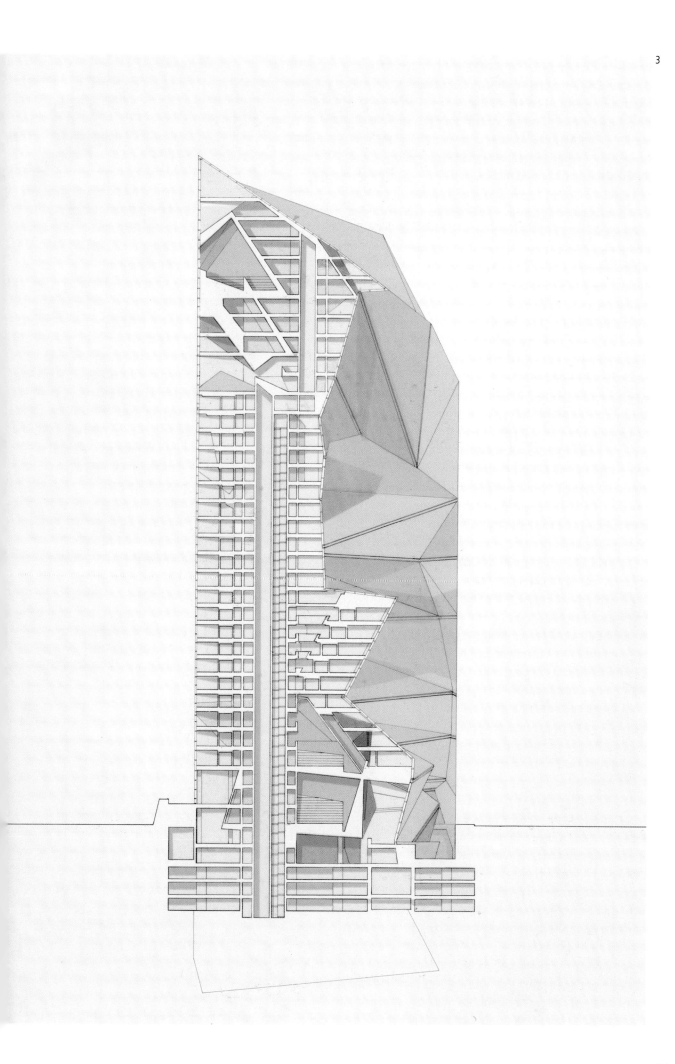

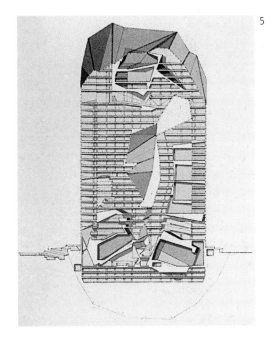

4 Computer rendering showing the tower
in its Berlin context.

5 Section a.

6 Aerial view from the east.

7 Site plan.

8 Presentation model from the west.

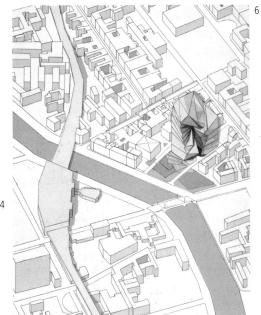

9

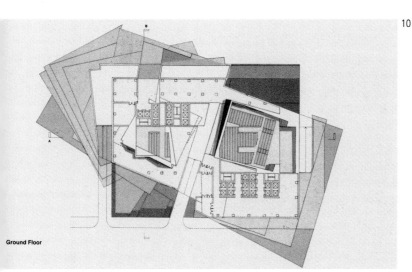

Ground Floor

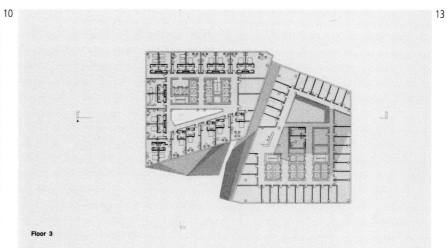

Floor 3

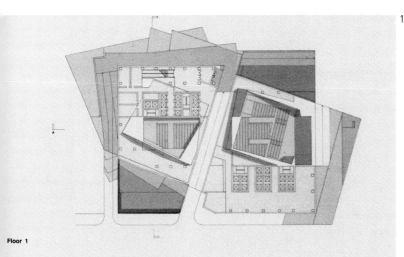

Floor 1

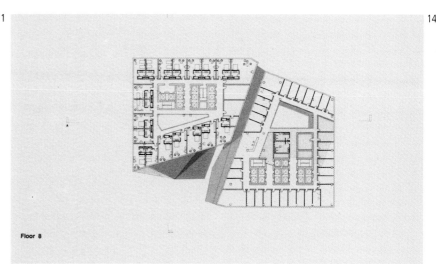

Floor 8

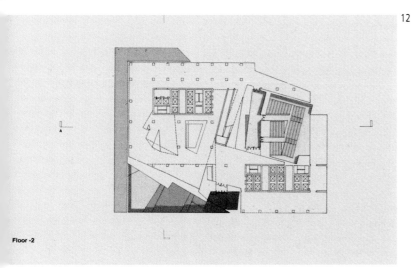

Floor -2

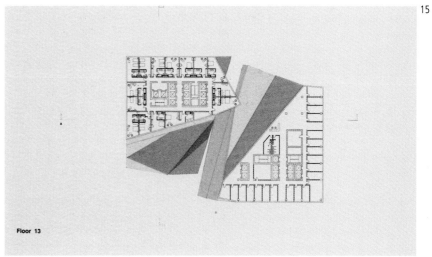

Floor 13

JACQUES HERZOG AND PIERRE DE MEURON

Herzog & de Meuron

Signal Box auf dem Wolf

Basel, Switzerland
Completed: 1994

In the midst of a train yard and next to the Basel engine depot, the Signal Box auf dem Wolf stands as a tall copper volume beside the eighteenth- and nineteenth-century walls of the Wolf-Gottesacker cemetery. Architects Jacques Herzog and Pierre de Meuron stacked workstations and electronic equipment for the control of signals to the surrounding depot and the related track of the Swiss Federal Railway on the building's six floors. The Signal Box evolved out of an interest in establishing a method of construction which roots itself in the chosen materials and thus shares a pragmatic connection with Herzog and de Meuron's earlier project for the Ricola Storage Facility (completed 1986).

Constructed of simple industrial materials, the Signal Box's concrete shell is insulated on the exterior and wrapped with copper strips approximately eight inches wide. These strips take the form of copper louvers that are twisted at certain locations in order to admit daylight to windows in the concrete walls behind them. By virtue of these repetitive louvers, the building acts as a Faraday cage, protecting the electronic equipment inside from unexpected external effects. Contrary to conventional practice in industrial buildings, the copper encasement disguises the floor divisions and obscures the scale of the building. As a result, the configuration establishes a specific relationship with the adjacent field of railway tracks, vividly expressing the physical qualities of the site.

The Signal Box stands amid mechanized surfaces at an industrial hub of modern transportation and is metaphorically and visually grounded in the particular conditions of the surrounds. The tracks and the rail yard represent a space of constant movement and confusion, for which the Signal Box provides an icon of stability. From across the tracks, the skin reads as a continuous copper volume, appearing as a reference point to center the divergent paths of movement. As a device, the building literally and metaphorically exerts control over the train cars. Moreover, the boxcar-shaped exterior volume and the facade's corrugation both evoke the surfaces of the trains in the nearby yards and the repetitive rails and ties of the surrounding tracks.

This rhythmic monotony of the tracks, mimicked by Herzog and de Meuron in the skin of the Signal Box, is counteracted by the animated reflections of the facades. The copper surfaces are such that they vary constantly, particularly given the modulating conditions of the context. At one moment, the structure stands as a continuous gleaming volume of copper; then — as the sun changes angles — striated shadows appear, thus emphasizing the banding that wraps across the four primary facades. Later, as the sun begins to set, the outlines of windows emerge from within the shadows, partially indicating the mysterious contents within. In this way, the exterior copper cladding animates what is otherwise an internally elemental building based on clear floor plans and sectional configurations.

1   View from across the railroad tracks.
Photo: Margherita Spiluttini.

2 Elevation detail.
   Photo: Margherita Spiluttini.
3 View at dusk.
   Photo: Margherita Spiluttini.

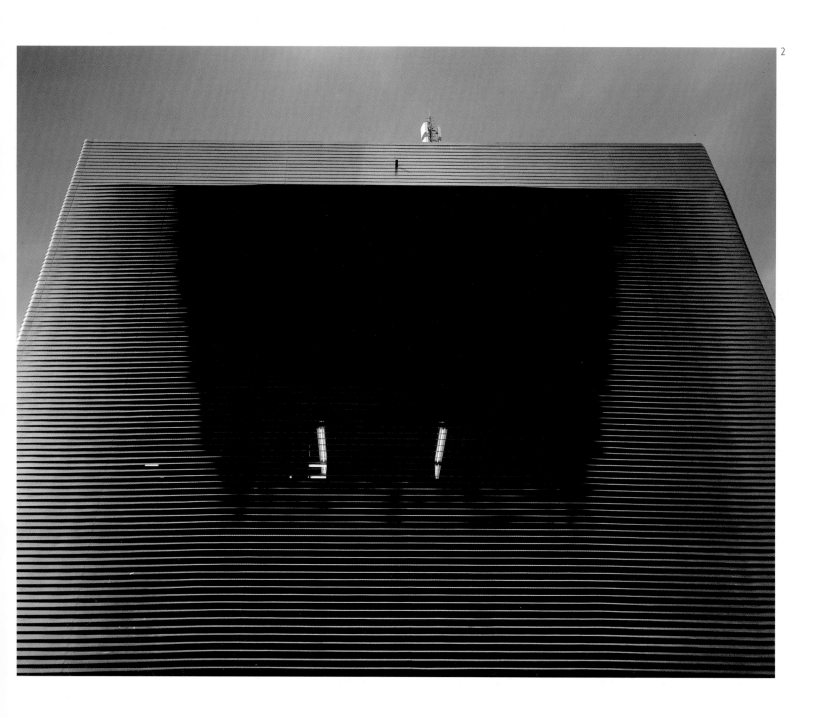

4 Frontal view from the train yard.
   Photo: Margherita Spiluttini.
5 View from across the railroad tracks.
   Photo: Margherita Spiluttini.

6   Presentation model.
     Photo: Studio Frei.
7   Presentation model.
     Photo: Studio Frei.

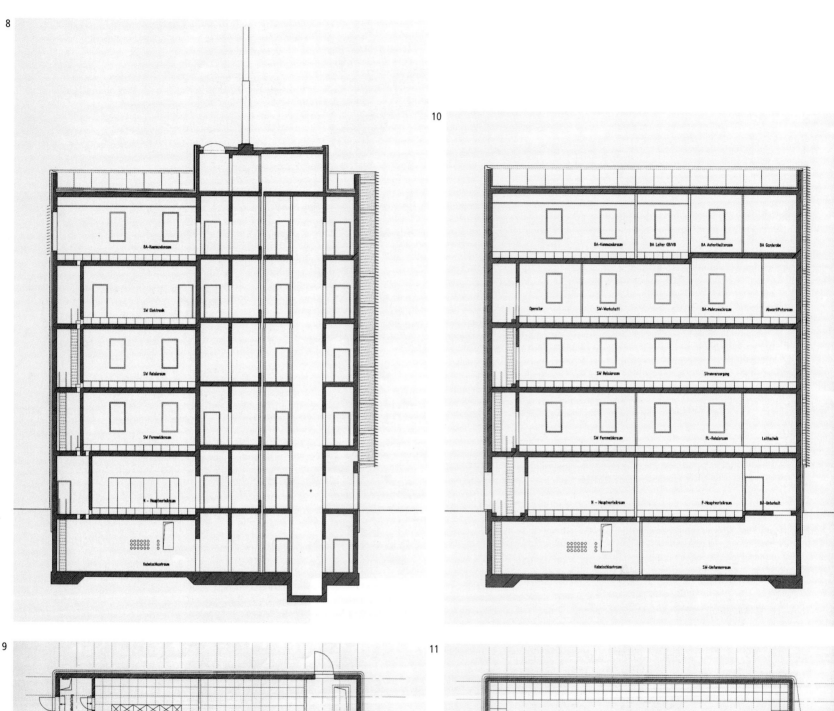

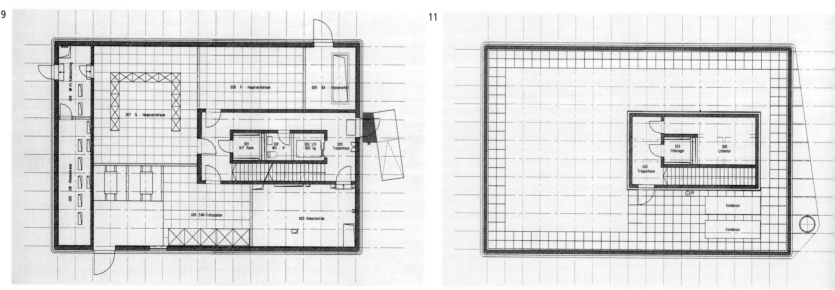

13

12

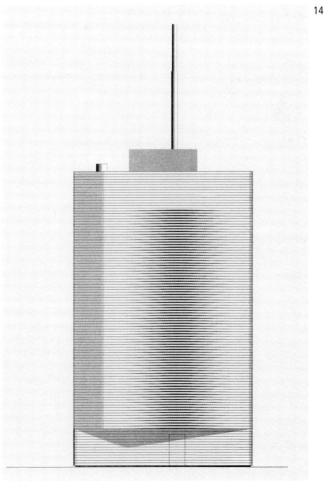

14

REM KOOLHAAS

Office for Metropolitan Architecture

Sea Terminal

Zeebrugge, Belgium
Competition: 1989

In order to maintain viability after the opening of the Channel Tunnel, the ferry companies operating across the English Channel proposed to make crossing that body of water more exciting. Not only would boats turn into floating entertainment worlds, but their destinations — the terminals — would shed their utilitarian character and become tourist attractions. To this effect, Rem Koolhaas designed the first-prize-winning competition entry for a terminal at the port of Zeebrugge, Belgium. In the architect's words, "[T]he project attempts to be at the same time fully artistic and totally efficient." Koolhaas developed the form as a sculptural object, independent of the functions it would contain, in order to resist classification and engender a series of associations: mechanical, industrial, utilitarian, abstract, poetic, surrealistic.

The imposing curve of the form contains a complex series of programs: a hotel, parking, offices, restaurants, a cinema, a pool, and a casino. Koolhaas fashioned a recognizable whole from a mix of facilities, loosely arranged shapes, and varied components, all housed within the terminal's singular form. A spiraling circulation system enables movement to occur without the need for intersections, thus handling divergent traffic types efficiently. Traffic forms on incoming and outgoing bands running parallel to the channel dike at the edge of the site.

The terminal's form is a cross between a sphere and a truncated cone. Containing ramps for service vehicles and automobiles, the two lowest floors organize traffic exiting and entering the ferries with maximum efficiency. Koolhaas projects that four ships could load and unload simultaneously without interrupting the traffic flow. Overhead, a multistory parking structure ascends in a spiral surrounding the central atrium, whose escalators and elevators culminate in a great public hall. From here, the panorama of sea and land is revealed for the first time. Halfway up the exterior elevation, this glass wall circumscribes the skin of the building and outwardly reveals the two levels of the hall containing public restaurants and bars.

Proceeding upwards, an internalized office tower in the shape of a wedge splits the cone into two vertical segments — housing the hotel and administrative offices, respectively — facing each other across a gap. This void offers an upward view to the sky and a downward view through a glass floor to the depths of the parking garage. Organized like a half-moon, the bank of hotel rooms is expressed on the exterior by porthole windows. Above this are the hotel lobby and its restaurant, as well as a movie theater whose panoramic screen is suspended above the spiraling central space and within the wedge-shaped void. The entire structure is capped by a casino, pool, and meeting rooms, all confined by an expansive glass dome. Under the dome, two independent islands connect across a central void by means of aerial ramps. On one side, the hotel roof terrace accommodates the casino. Opposite, an amphitheater rests atop the administrative complex and doubles as a conference center, sloping down toward the sea.

Concerned with injecting a new landmark into the landscape, Koolhaas chose a conceptual theme he entitled "a working Babel." Like the original Babel, his proposed terminal represents both the ambition and the chaos of a society embarking on a unified future. But Koolhaas expects his machine to avoid the original Babel's failure through its function, its ability to welcome, entertain, and effortlessly sort travelers on land and sea.

Note
The quotation from Rem Koolhaas was taken from a project text provided by the architect.

1   Plaster massing model.
     Photo: Hans Werlemann.

2 Rendered elevation.
3 Plaster model in a gallery installation.
   Photo: Hans Werlemann.

4   Waterside view of the presentation model.
    Photo: Hans Werlemann.
5   Aerial view of the presentation model.
    Photo: Hans Werlemann.
6   Aerial view of the site model.
    Photo: Hans Werlemann.

4

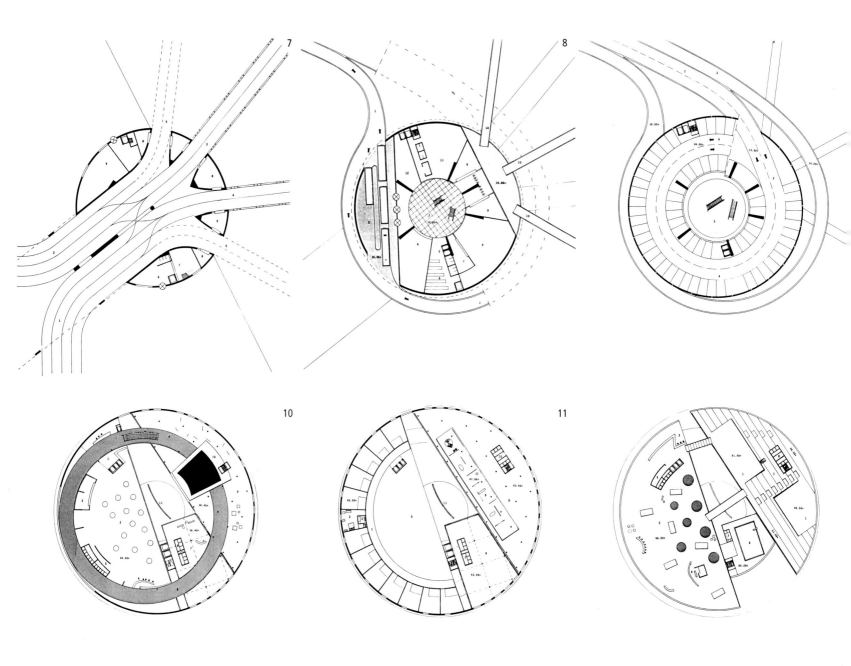

13 Section through the offices.
14 Section through the hotel and cinema.
15 North-east elevation.
16 North-west elevation.

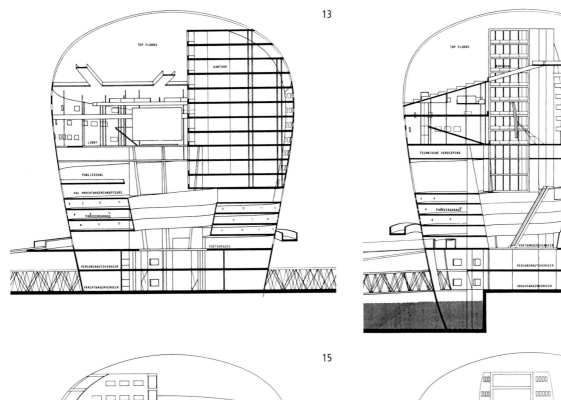

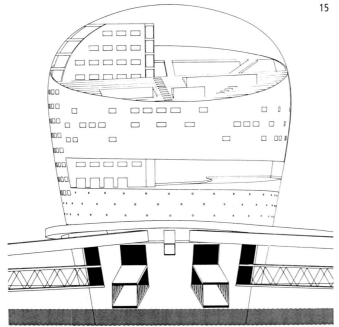

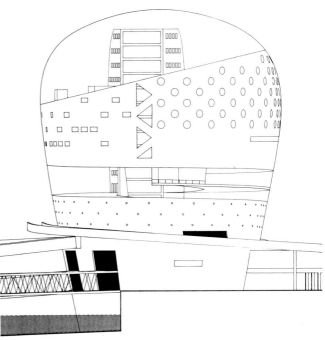

RAFAEL MONEO
José Rafael Moneo, Architect

Kursaal Cultural Center and Auditorium

San Sebastián, Spain
Construction commenced: 1995

The city of San Sebastián owes much of its exceptional beauty to the surrounding natural landscape. Few cities can claim a more favorable environment. The site of the Kursaal Cultural Center and Auditorium at the mouth of the Urumea River is a geographical accident that Rafael Moneo wishes to retain. Hence, the architect proposed to erect a building that would not violate the presence of the river in the city. Constituting the key programmatic elements, the auditorium and conference hall are conceived as separate, autonomous volumes, as two gigantic rocks stranded at the mouth of the river and forming part of the landscape rather than belonging to the city. All other facilities — including the exhibition halls, meeting rooms, offices, a restaurant, and musicians' services — are located in the platform at the base of these cubes.

The auditorium contained within the larger of the two prismatic volumes measures approximately 200 by 160 by 90 feet and celebrates the notion of a geographical accident by inclining slightly toward the sea. The volume of the two-thousand-seat auditorium is inscribed asymmetrically inside the glass prism, seeming to float within it. Moneo oriented the asymmetry such that a visitor entering the foyer is unconsciously led toward the highest level, enabling views of Mount Urgull and the sea in all its splendor through a singular window. This window punctures the building's double wall, composed of a steel skeleton clad inside and out with laminated glass elements. The result is a neutral and luminous interior space whose only contact with the outside world is through the foyer window.

Outside, the glass surfaces protect against salt-laden winds from the sea, making the volume a dense, opaque, yet changing mass by day and a mysterious source of light by night. According to Moneo, the rectangular hall adheres to the formula deemed best by acoustical technicians, with dimensions nearly that of a square in terms of its length-to-width ratio, a flat ceiling, and a height that makes for a volume of approximately 360 cubic feet per spectator. In this case, the novelty lies in the continuity and free-standing condition of the hall, providing access to all areas from any of the doors. The architect employed similar design and structural criteria in planning the smaller conference hall, which he also inscribed in an inclined prism, in this case measuring 140 by 120 by 80 feet. Though less evident in its asymmetry, the view from the foyer to Mount Ulía and the sea beyond is equally spectacular.

Below these two cubes, the platform provides entrances to the auditorium and conference hall and the information and ticket booths, as well as access to a 720-car parking structure. This plinth also serves as the meeting space between the cultural center and the city, opening onto Zoriola Avenue and forming a wide outdoor space for public access. In this manner, Moneo intends the new cultural center to be a significant urban episode in what has always been a dramatic stretch between Mount Ulía and Mount Igueldo.

1   Aerial View of the presentation model
    from the riverside. Photo: Lluis Casals.

2 Waterside view of the presentation model.
  Photo: Lluís Casals.
3 Photomontage.

2

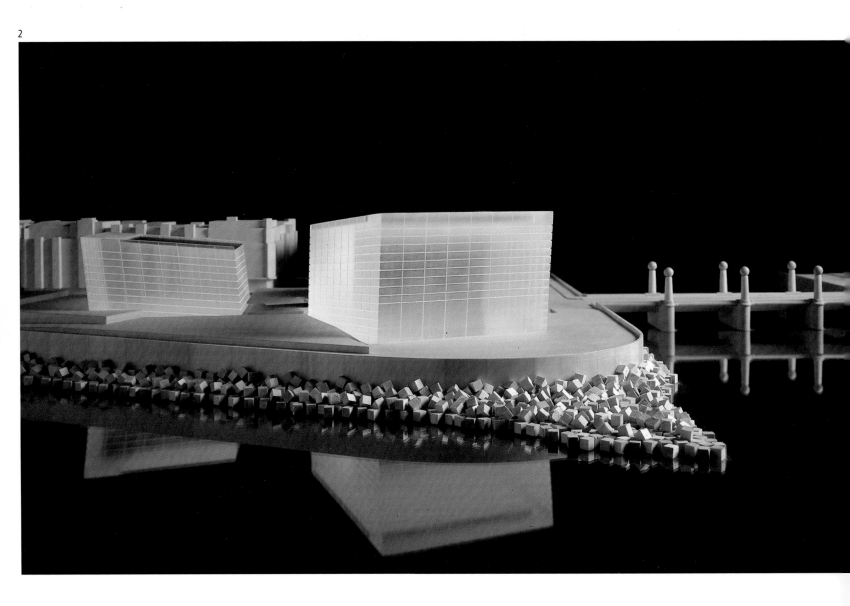

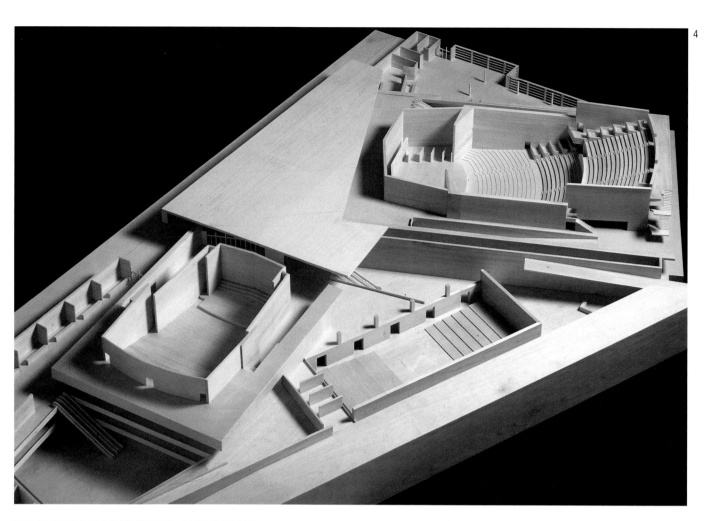

4 Ground-plan model.
   Photo: Lluís Casals.
5 Auditorium sectional model.
   Photo: Céasar San Millán.
6 Waterside view of
   the presentation model.
   Photo: J. Belzunce.
7 Presentation model
   from the river.
   Photo: Lluís Casals.

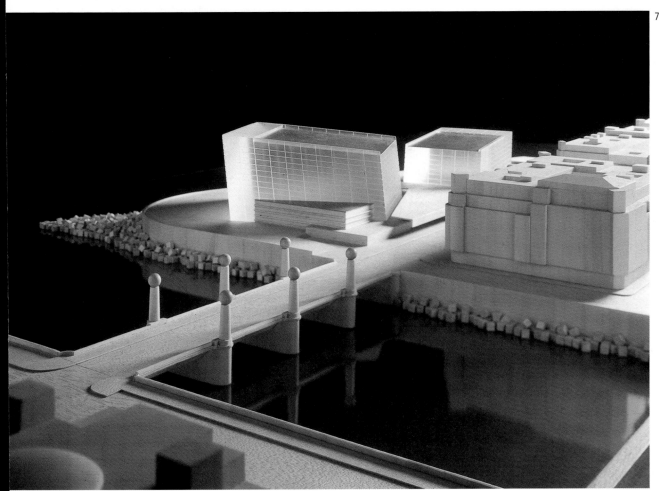

8 Ground-floor plan.
9 Second-floor plan.

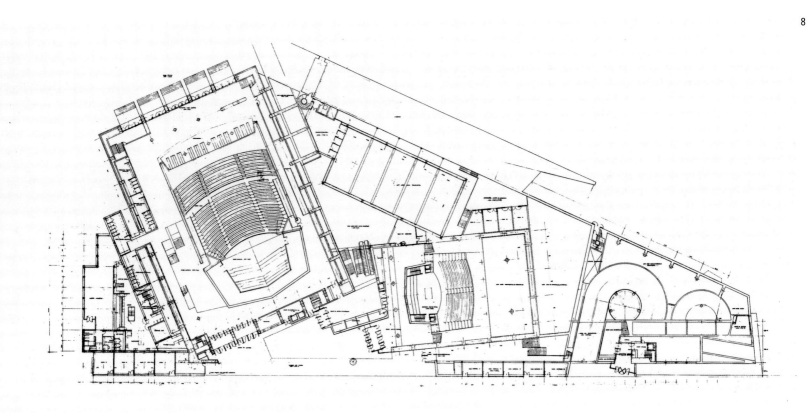

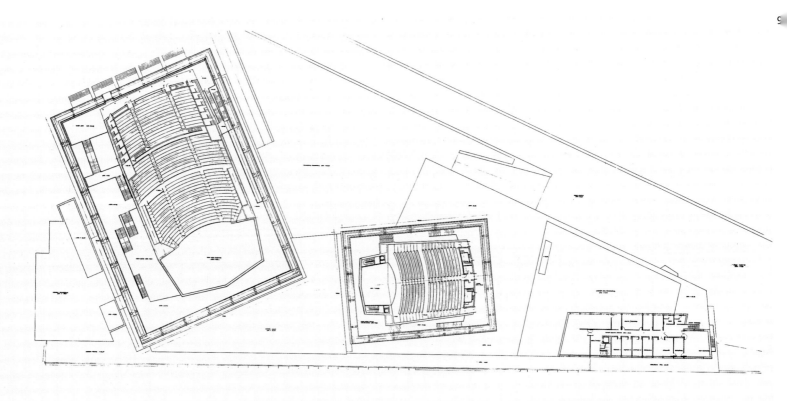

10 Transversal section through the auditorium.
11 Longitudinal section through the auditorium.

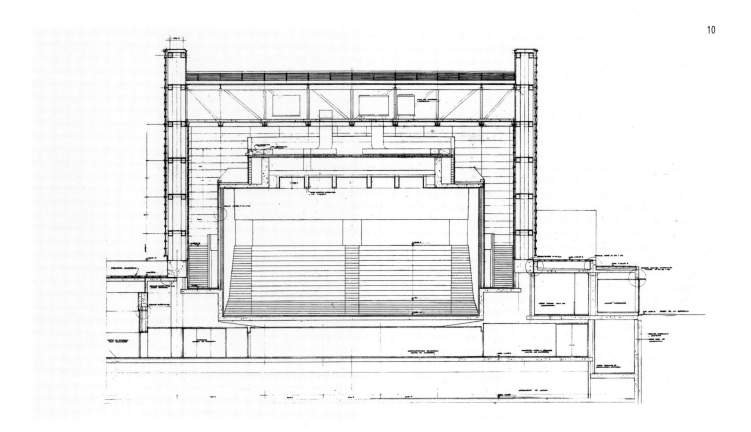

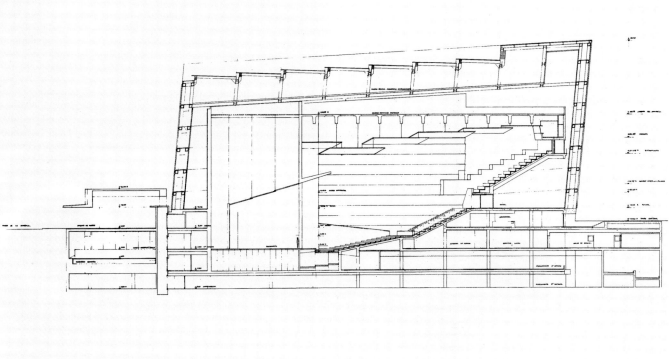

12 Exterior wall mock-up.
   Photo: César San Millán.
13 Waterfront elevation.
14 Auditorium skin details.

12

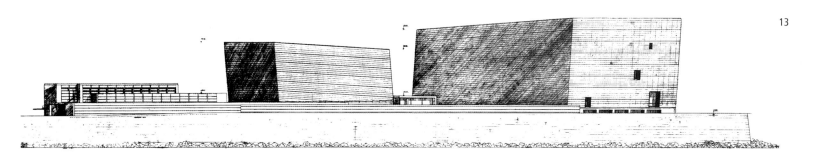

13

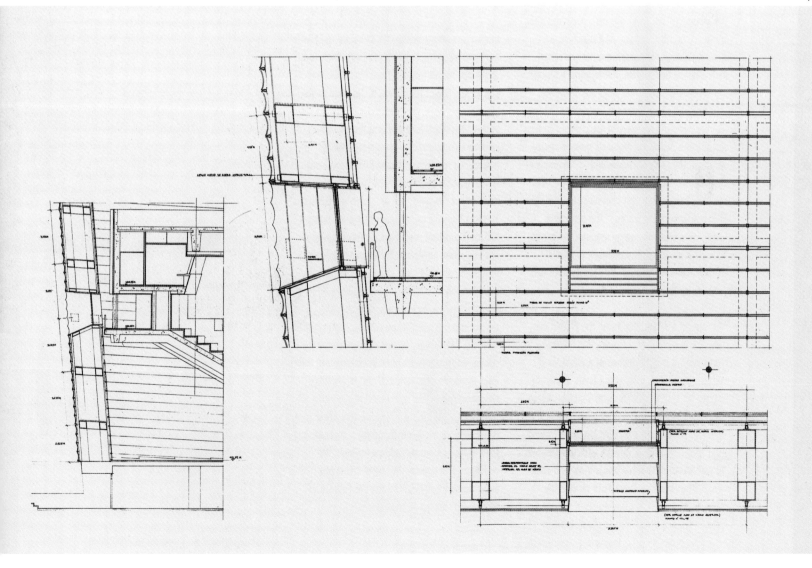

Yokohama International Port Terminal
Yokohama, Japan
Construction to commence: 1997

The competition-winning proposal for the Yokohama International Port Terminal is the first major commission for designers Farshid Moussavi and Alejandro Zaera-Polo, collectively known as Foreign Office Architects. Covering an area roughly 1,500 feet (extending northward into Japan's largest harbor) by 230 feet, the self-contained facilities will accommodate the transfer of passengers between massive international cruise ships and the city of Yokohama.

The architects' strategy calls for a seamless integration of space, program, and structure, all defined through topographic variations rather than physical boundaries. The terminal's topography weaves together two separate networks: Yokohama's public system of waterfront spaces and the flowing pathways of the cruise-ship passengers. The architects replaced symbolic gateways and traditional borders with a "machine of integration," allowing passengers and pedestrians alike to move almost imperceptibly through different subjective "states." The proposed spaces minimize the energy required to change state — from that of local citizen to that of world traveler — through their continuous and gradual variation in form.

At the most fundamental level, the project consists of one surface that breaks into four programmatic strata. Composed of a plaza, a garden, an exhibition court, and a traffic zone, the uppermost level penetrates into Yokohama Bay, converting water into an inhabitable space. Understood as an extension of the city's ground level, this surface joins directly with the adjacent Yamashita Park to form a major L-shaped urban space. Moussavi and Zaera-Polo located the terminal itself, as well as glass-encased shops, restaurants, and a major civic space, beneath this expansive public surface. Below are service facili-

ties and a concrete parking structure. Construction is specified almost entirely in steel, with the exterior plaza covered in anti-corrosive plastic grills similar to those used on oil rigs. In a conscious attempt to avoid a segmented system of support characterized by columns, walls, or floors, Moussavi and Zaera-Polo integrated the structure within the surfaces of the terminal by means of pleats or folds in the floor plates. These creases define spaces, direct pathways, and accommodate ramps from one level to the next.

In effect, the team sought to associate the building's prominent global functions with their local urban counterparts. Consequently, public amenities for the city of Yokohama are located at the tip of the terminal in order to encourage an interaction between the citizen and the traveler. Likened to a battlefield, constantly shifting boundaries result from changes in the volume of space required by the carriers. To facilitate this demand for flexibility, the architects envisioned a system of mobile or collapsible physical barriers, allowing constant reconfigurations of the borderlines between territories. Pedestrian movement from Yokohama's streets connects smoothly to the boarding level of the terminal. From there, it bifurcates to produce a multiplicity of paths, thus magnifying the intensity of walking through the building. The primary system of circulation interconnects the pathways of both citizens and travelers by means of a series of circulatory loops. Passengers enter the terminal through a slice in the upper plaza's surface, proceeding either to a check-in zone for domestic travel or through customs stations for international voyages. The architects aim to intensify these events and sequences by emphasizing the coexistence of global and local pedestrian networks.

1   Perspective of the terminal interior.

2 Photomontage showing the port.
3 Terminal's upper surface.

2

4   Terminal's upper surface.
5   Cruise deck.
6   Salon of Civic Exchange.
7   Apron level.

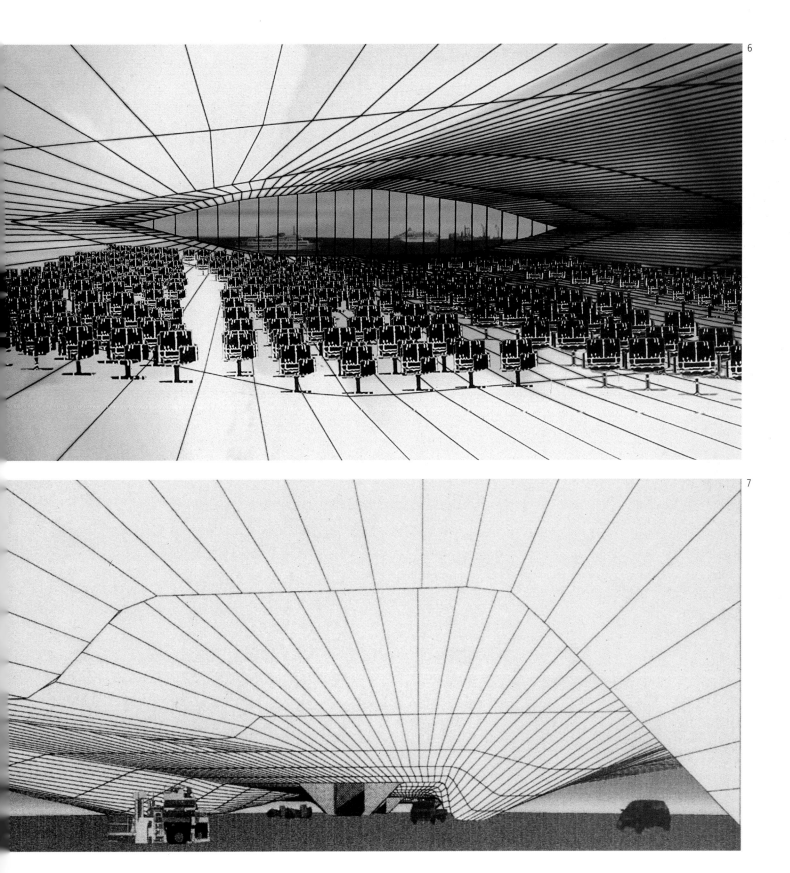

8   Molds used for model production.
9   Model.

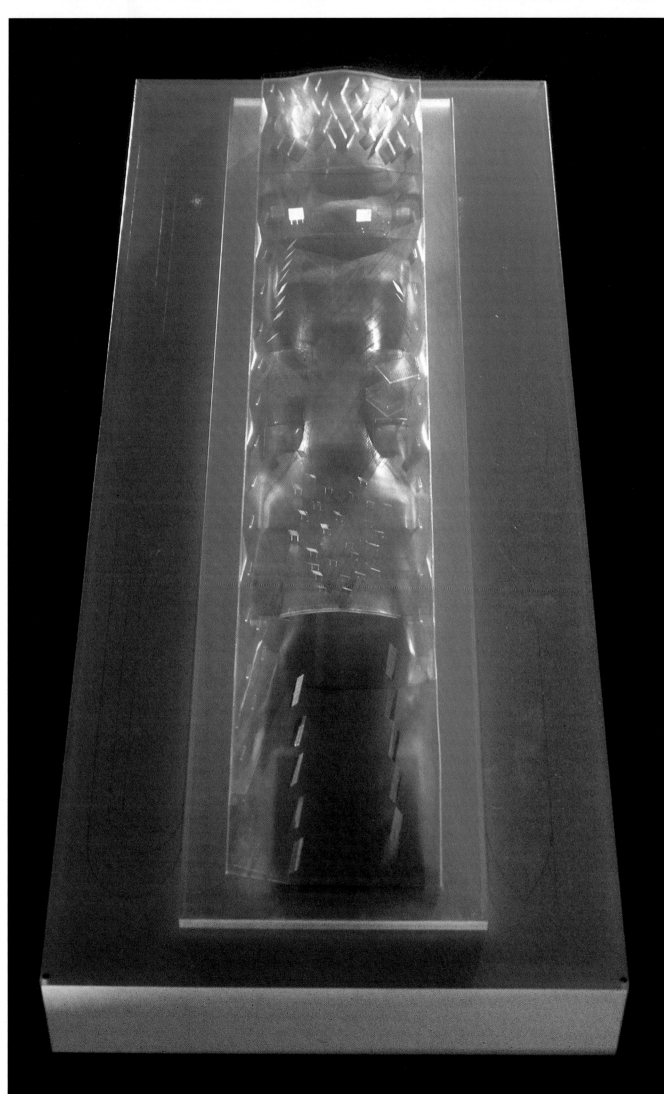

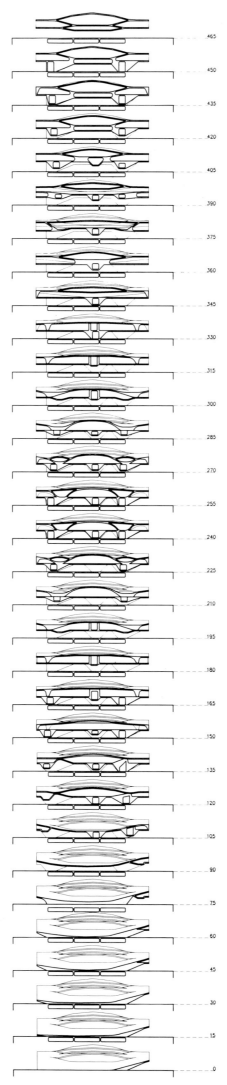

465
450
435
420
405
390
375
360
345
330
315
300
285
270
255
240
225
210
195
180
165
150
135
120
105
90
75
60
45
30
15
0

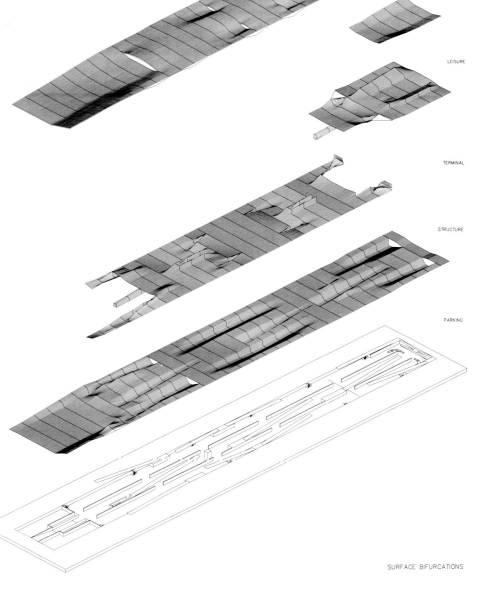

PLAZA

CIVIC EXCHANGE

LEISURE

TERMINAL

STRUCTURE

PARKING

SURFACE BIFURCATIONS

10 Transversal sections.

11 Axonometric series showing surface bifurcations.

12 Ground-floor plan.

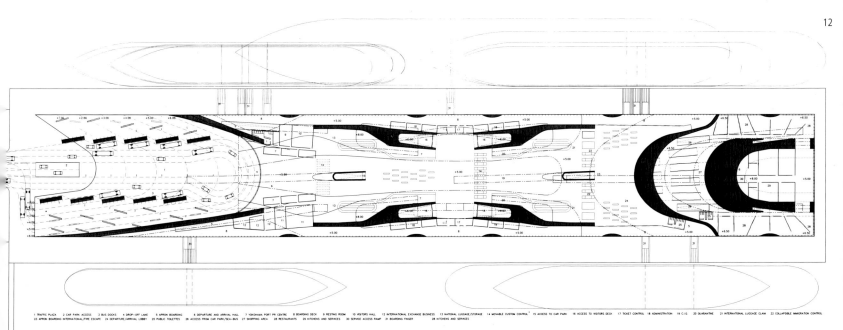

1 TRAFFIC PLAZA   2 CAR PARK ACCESS   3 BUS DOCKS   4 DROP-OFF LANE   5 APRON BOARDING   6 DEPARTURE AND ARRIVAL HALL   7 YOKOHAMA PORT PR CENTRE   8 BOARDING DECK   9 RESTING ROOM   10 VISITORS HALL   12 INTERNATIONAL EXCHANGE BUSINESS   13 NATIONAL LUGGAGE/STORAGE   14 MOVABLE CUSTOM CONTROL   15 ACCESS TO CAR PARK   16 ACCESS TO VISITORS DECK   17 TICKET CONTROL   18 ADMINISTRATION   19 C.I.Q   20 QUARANTINE   21 INTERNATIONAL LUGGAGE CLAIM   22 COLLAPSIBLE IMMIGRATION CONTROL   23 APRON BOARDING INTERNATIONAL/FIRE ESCAPE   24 DEPARTURE/ARRIVAL LOBBY   25 PUBLIC TOILETTES   26 ACCESS FROM CAR PARK/SEA-BUS   27 SHOPPING AREA   28 RESTAURANTS   29 KITCHENS AND SERVICES   30 SERVICE ACCESS RAMP   31 BOARDING FINGER   28 KITCHENS AND SERVICES

Farshid Moussavi and Alejandro Zaera-Polo 123

13 Aerial view of the terminal's upper surface.

14 Perspectives of the bifurcated sequences.

13

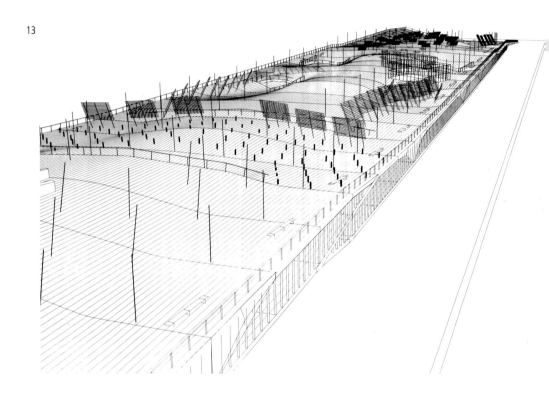

14

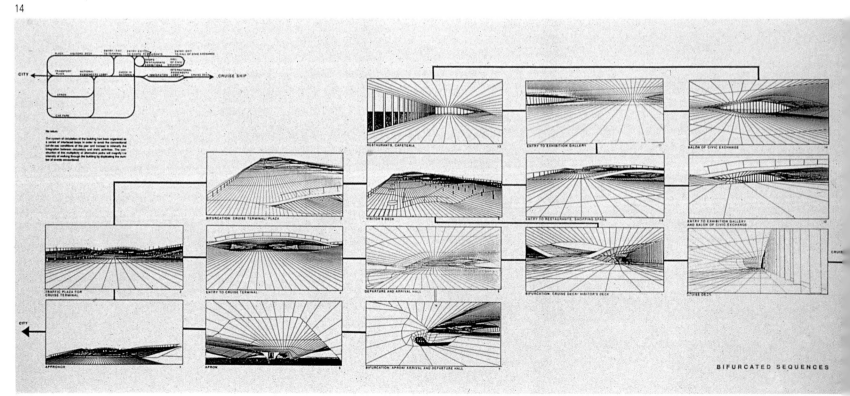

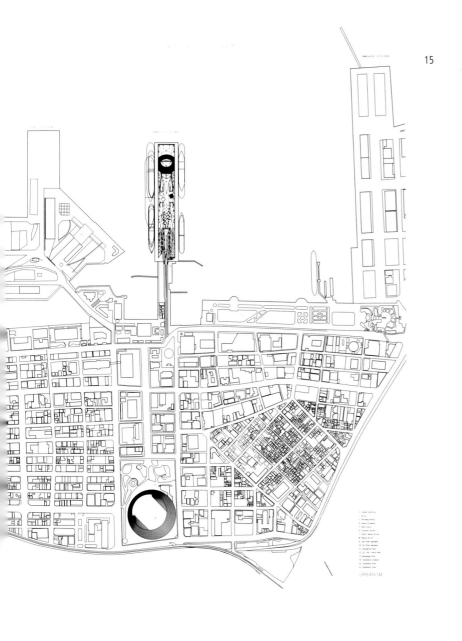

15 Site plan.
16 Perspectives of the harbor-side elevation.

16

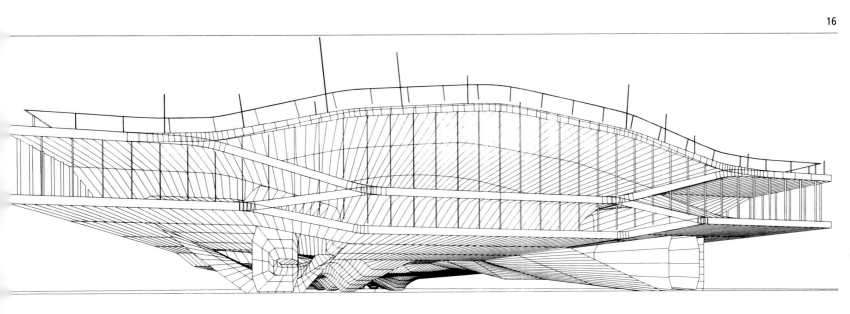

Farshid Moussavi and Alejandro Zaera-Polo **125**

The New National Theater

Tokyo, Japan
Competition: 1986

As a singular, enigmtic form, Jean Nouvel's submittal for the New National Theater competition stands in sharp contrast to Tokyo's intricate buildings and electrified advertisements. The smooth, highly polished exterior surface appears as a giant black granite volume, slightly inflated at one end and perforated at its center by two large carvings into the stone. These, in turn, partially reveal the hidden workings of the project: a small, a medium, and a large auditorium as well as a central public hall. Nouvel's design scheme results in a theatrical architecture experienced as an instrument of both cultural and social spectacle.

The wavy outline of the mirrored New National Theater stands higher and broader than its surrounding buildings and masks the three auditoria within. Nouvel treated each as an object, an instrument of sorts encased by the singular granite box. Rectangular in shape with rounded edges, the smallest space occupies the uppermost portion of the building. The two others appear as expanded conglomerations of multiple volumes with slight inclinations; both end up afloat in the huge space of the main vestibule. Precious in nature and formed from elegant materials (wood, brass, and leather), these "instruments" are protected by their countershaped case, equivalent to a gigantic shiny (and evidently hollow) stone that outwardly reflects the sky and city. From the surrounding streets, the mysterious contents are visible through the symmetrical openings in either side elevation. These also serve to project the internal ceremony of the spaces outward to the city.

Public access to the building from street level occurs through three very wide and low doors at the monolith's base. Entering, one moves past a chamfered wall approximately 30 feet thick that houses service facilities. Still encased in black and shiny surfaces, the ground-floor entry hall is flat and massive and surrounds a ticket office and information desk. Two facing stairs — disproportionately large compared to the scale of the entry hall — rise suddenly and unexpectedly upwards to the floor of the central vestibule, a space over 160 feet in height.

In moving between these two spaces, the theater patron experiences a sudden shift of position, standing all at once at the base of the two wide stairs, each sandwiched between escalators, and beneath the vast central void. Walls and ceiling are still fashioned of the now-familiar black granite; however, three golden volumes — the auditoria — hover above the space, suspended from the massive granite walls. This main space looks out to the city and sky through two enormous glass openings, approximately 100 feet high by 65 feet wide, each equipped with a sliding granite panel. An access stair crosses diagonally in front of this opening, reaffirming the monumental scale of the void.

Nouvel devoted a significant portion of the lobby to a restaurant and its facilities, above which he suspended the largest auditorium. Entering this theater requires moving through a network of stairs and passages. Once inside, materials change from stone to mahogany, leather, and brass. The proscenium and stage constitute the inside of the metaphoric instrument, a space whose furnishings were designed by Philippe Starck. Eight levels of vaulted balconies align along the outer edge of this largest volume. Here, walls and surfaces are flexible and adjust to the needs of a given performance. The medium-sized auditorium employs the same materials, but all surfaces are fixed. The smallest hall acts as a multipurpose theater, essentially a convertible laboratory entirely surrounded by technology. Nouvel's unbuilt New National Theater, then, combines internal flexibility with external stasis.

1   West elevation.

2

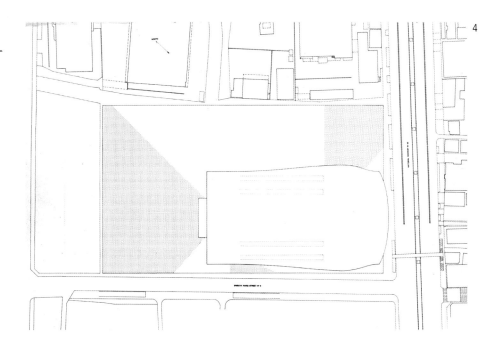

4

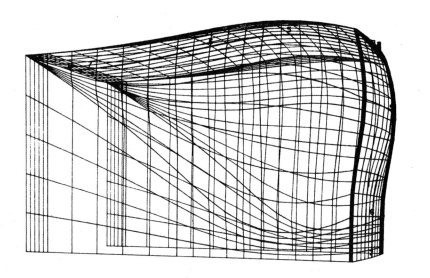

5

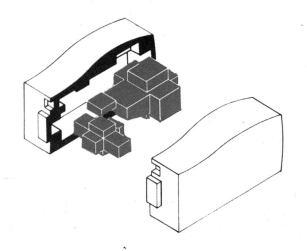

6

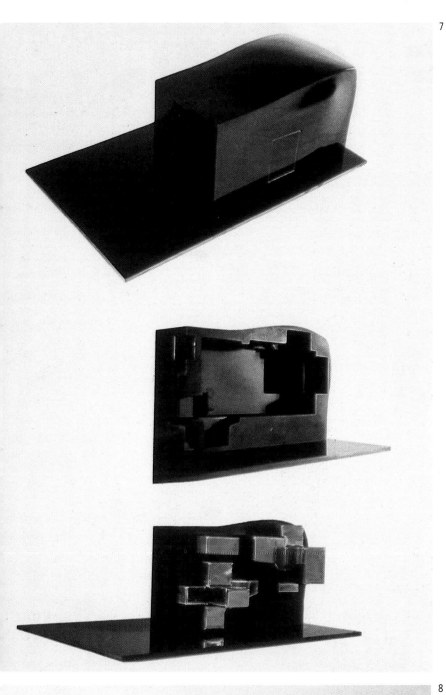

4   Site plan.
5   Computer model of topographic surfaces.
6   Axonometric diagram of the volumes.
7   Presentation model showing the interior volumes.
8   Presentation model.

9   Ground-floor plan.
10 Lobby-level plan.
11 Medium-sized auditorium floor plan.
12 Main auditorium floor plan.

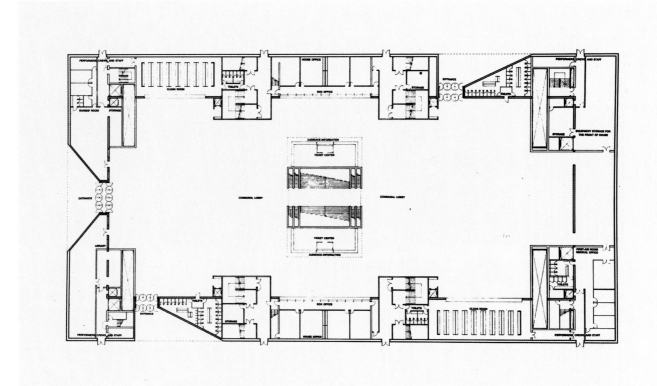

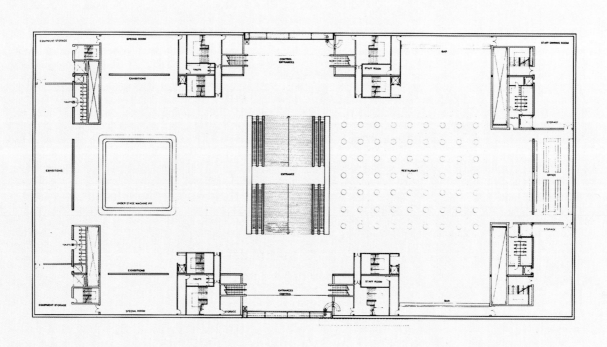

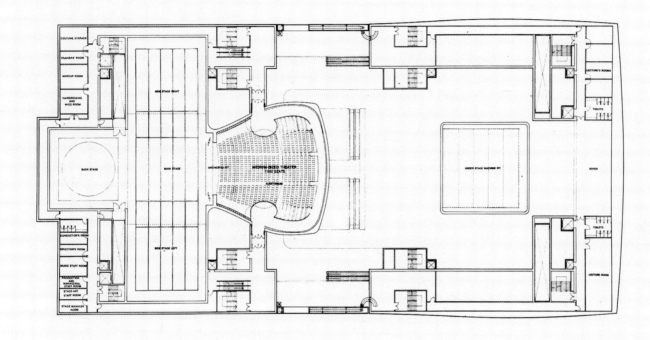

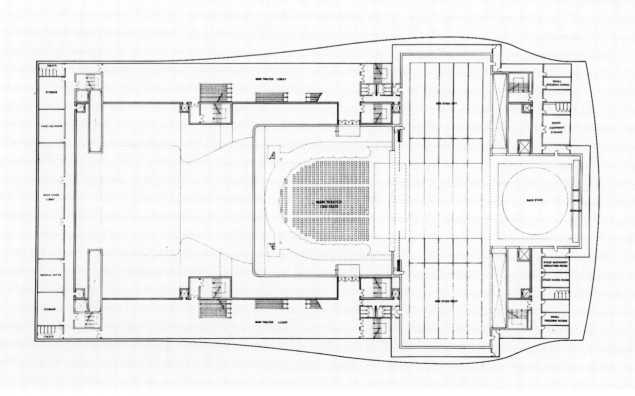

13 Perspective of the communal lobby.

14 Transversal section.

15 Longitudinal section.

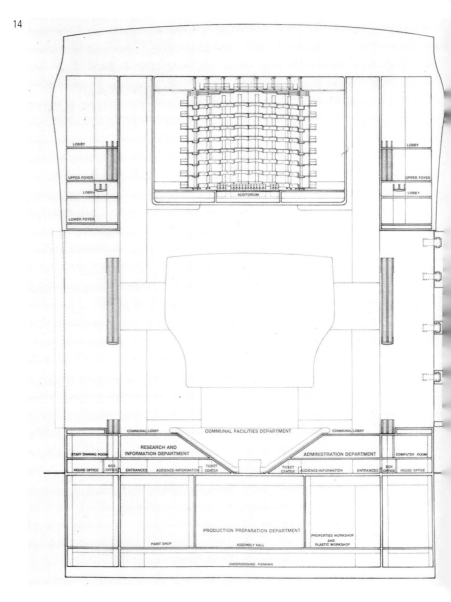

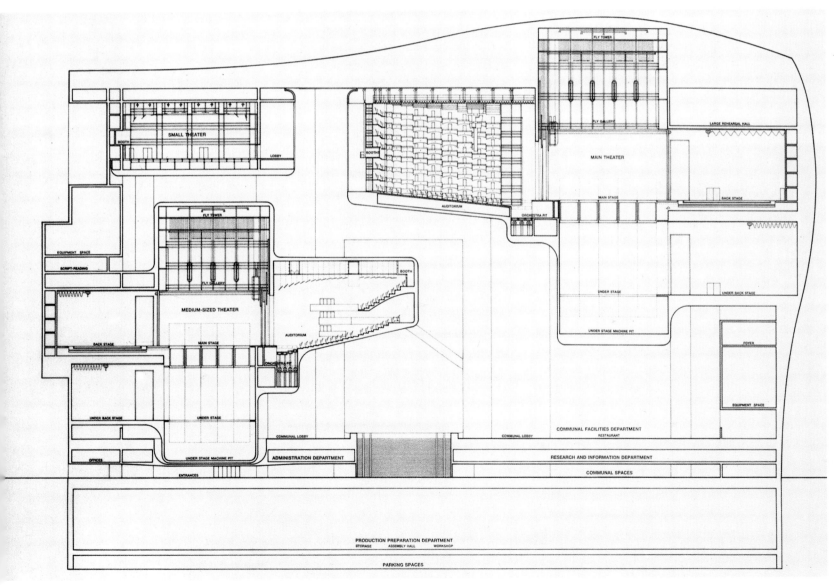

PHILIPPE SAMYN
Samyn and Partners

Walloon Forestry Department Shell
Marche-en-Famenne, Belgium
Completed: 1995

The Forestry Department Shell at Marche-en-Famenne, Belgium, houses facilities for the processing and treatment of seeds coming from the Ardennes Forest and the surrounding Walloon region. Positioned in a polygonal clearing and surrounded by bicentenary oaks, the building consolidates the multiple programmatic needs of the Belgian agency under one continuous ovoid shell. Philippe Samyn was particularly concerned with the ecological impact and economy of the structure. As a result, he designed the building using rigorous experimental analyses as well as sophisticated construction techniques based on laboratory testing of the structural behavior of various woods.

The building is essentially composed of a workshop, a series of cold storage areas, and a few offices and laboratories, all of which are contained beneath a single glass and wood shell. This main ovoidal volume occupies a footprint of approximately 180 by 90 feet and stands about 40 feet high. The internal workshop forms around a central aisle for pre-drying and grain treatment. Here, the seed-processing machinery is stored. Located inside the shell along its longitudinal edges, two secondary buildings contain seed-cooling chambers, storage, administrative offices, and small laboratories. These concrete-block volumes serve to stabilize the arches of the main external structure and provide thermal insulation and fireproofing for the stored materials.

The external structure consists of a framework of double-layered wooden arches, all clamped at their edges by the reinforced concrete platform. The basic unit of this shell structure is a double-layered arch composed of various rectangular steam-bent pieces of wood of small sections (two by four inches up to three by six inches), all approximately twenty feet in length. The complete span of the arch is formed from a series of circular segments which, when joined, approximate a funicular curve, the axes of which are implanted in radial planes forming a torus section. Coupled with the use of computer design techniques, this arrangement effectively reduces costs by standardizing the wooden sections.

The resultant shell is entirely clad in 1,691 panels of laminated glass with a slightly reflective and neutral coating, providing a layer of protection from the elements. Each panel is attached to thin aluminum arches that straddle the transversal load-bearing system. This is where Samyn's design breaks with conventional greenhouses. The building's wooden arches not only provide the structural support for the glass enclosure but also minimize heat gain in the central spaces through their cumulative shading effect. The wooden structure aids the ventilation system by absorbing and reflecting heat at the glass surface.

Viewed from the outside, the repetitive glass and wooden elements distort the surrounding environment, while light and color are reflected in smoothly modulating patterns across the ribbed skin. Still, the glass only partially masks the more intricate cage of wood beneath. Depending on lighting conditions and angles of view, the building appears either as a hermetic shell or, in contradiction, as a lacework of wood which alludes to the more complex internal organization of the various functional components.

1   View from the woods.
    Photo: Bastin & Evrad.

2   Computer-modeling view of the exterior.
    Image: Star Info.
3   Computer-modeling view of the interior.
    Image: Star Info.
4   Computer-modeling view of the exterior.
    Image: Star Info.

2

5　Exterior view.
　　Photo: Bastin & Evrard.
6　Presentation model.
　　Photo: Bauters Sprl.

5

7

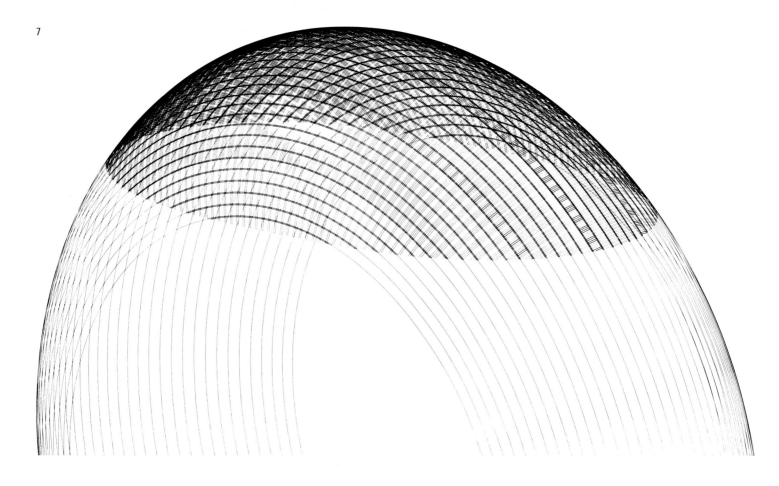

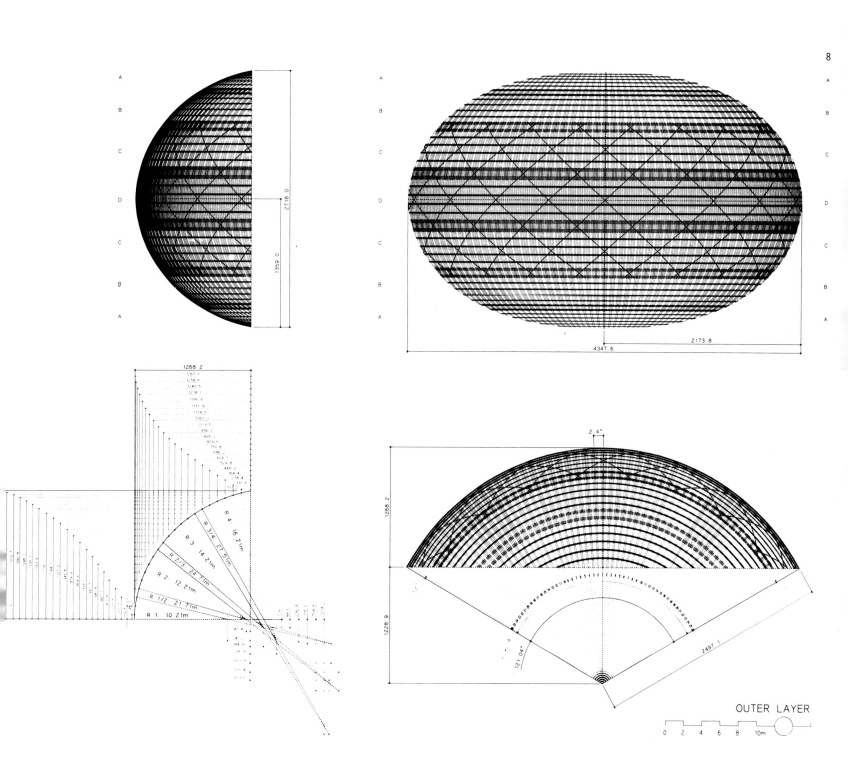

8

OUTER LAYER

0 2 4 6 8 10m

9   Longitudinal section detail.
10 Floor plan.
11 Site plan.
12 Elevations.

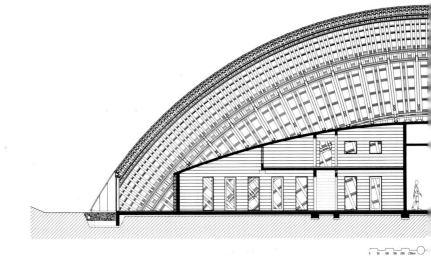

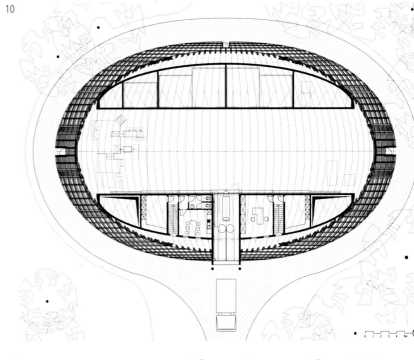

10

11

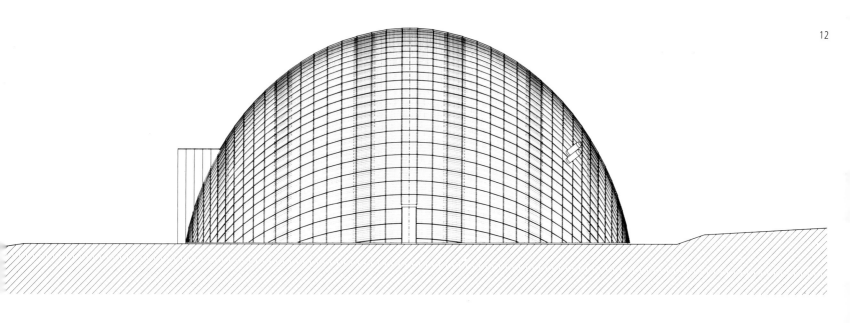

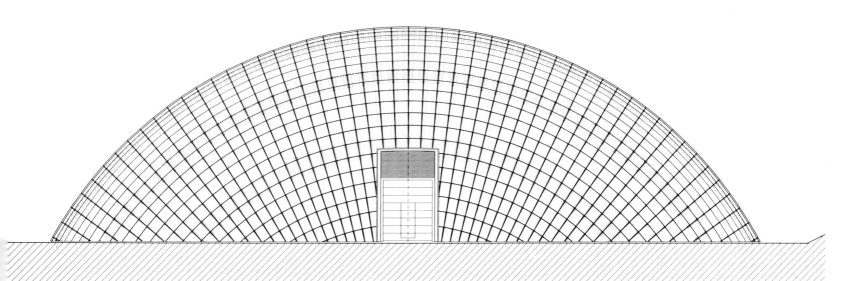

13

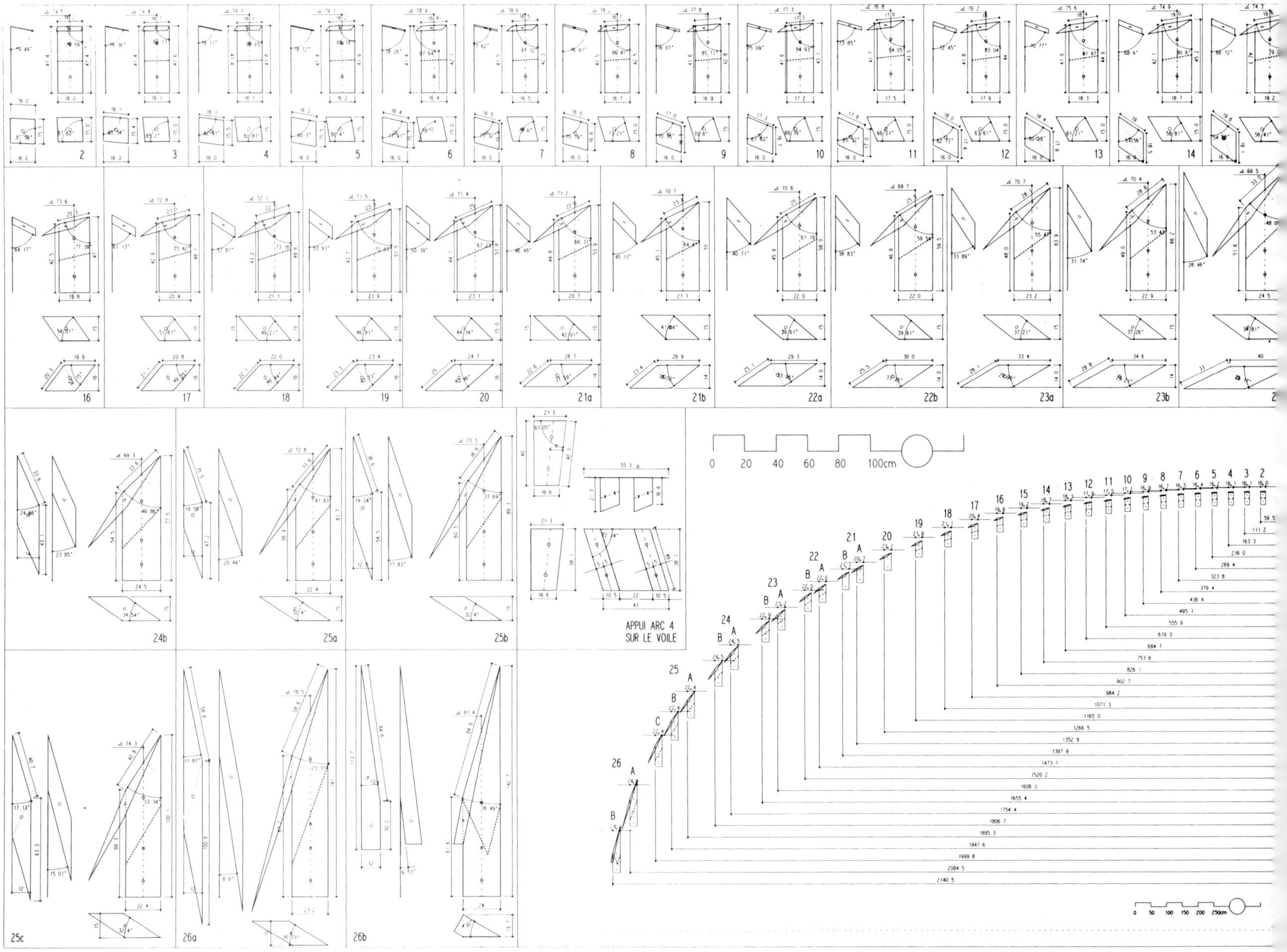
APPUI ARC 4
SUR LE VOILE
0 20 40 60 80 100cm
0 50 100 150 200 250cm
16
17
18
19
20
21a
21b
22a
22b
23a
23b
24b
25a
25b
25c
26a
26b

12

13 Construction details of the wooden sections.
14 Interior during construction.
15 Interior during construction.
16 Interior detailed view.
17 Side entry. Photo: Bastin & Evrard.

PHILIPPE STARCK

Starck

The Baron Vert

Osaka, Japan
Completed: 1992

Wedged between two vastly different urban environments in Osaka, Philippe Starck's Baron Vert mediates the congested thoroughfare it faces and a field of tombstones at its back. Starck's building is strategically inserted at the junction of the dense modern city and the old quarter represented by the nearby pagoda roofs. The structure negotiates among the static granite monuments and the fast-paced cars, buses, and pedestrians; it stands midway between a contemplative cemetery and an active street-scape.

It was not for lack of alternate sites that the architect painstakingly chose the thin, irregular plot. In fact, Starck visited nearly a dozen venues with the president of the developing company Meisei. Rather, it was the metaphoric qualities of the chosen site that ultimately caught the designer's attention. To suit it, he invented an architecture that straddles the border between the tranquillity of a city for the dead and the ceaseless activity of a living urban center. In typical fashion, the designer initially christened his project the Baron Rouge, recalling the German fighter pilot whose innovative flying style similarly straddled life and death. Consequently, the aviator's green-skinned namesake (changed to red's complementary color by Starck to heighten the sense of elegance) offers a protective barrier between two equally disparate built conditions.

In completing the project, Starck designed a pair of buildings markedly different in their surface treatments. Fashioned from green metallic panels that mask a reinforced concrete and steel structure, the primary building houses open-plan office space. Starck molded the exterior skin of this wedge-shaped volume, sculpting two austere faces interrupted by bladelike windows with canted glass panes. By virtue of their angle, these windows are invisible to the pedestrian below

and appear only as indentations in an otherwise continuously paneled surface. The smaller concrete building behind shares material and volumetric characteristics with the adjacent stone tombs. Sharp-edged and cubic, its shape opposes the molded surfaces of its green companion, while its circular windows echo the Japanese characters that align vertically along the surfaces of each gravestone.

The contradictory nature of the exterior treatments of these two buildings is, however, muted on the interior. Used as commercial office spaces on seven levels, the interior surfaces are finished with concrete walls and wooden floors. Starck designed the public amenities as well, including all kitchenettes, the entrance lobby, and various facilities scattered throughout the building. Through this design process, he aimed to transform work spaces into spaces for theatrical living, into places of illusion. Entering the lobby from the street level, one descends into the two story hall by means of a staircase that doubles as an arched bridge. The city outside is revealed through large expanses of glass on the two elongated sides of the Baron Vert. In effect, Starck created a space that is suspended above the field of burial stones and simultaneously entrenched deep below the neighboring street.

As an urban strategist, Starck has been credited with aiming for a "conglomeration of out-of-scale objects, full of energy and vitality." Here and in his earlier Tokyo projects, Asahi (1990) and Nani Nani (1989), Starck conceived of his buildings as monumental figures which he playfully imposed upon the city. He imagines future cities will be composed "like a game of chess, of surrealist or Dada objects," thus embodying metaphoric and formal qualities similar to those evoked by the Baron Vert.

Note
The quotations were taken from: Philippe Starck, *Philippe Starck* (Cologne, Benedikt Taschen, 1991), pp. 26, 28.

1   Rear elevation from the cemetery.
    Photo: Nacasa & Partners.

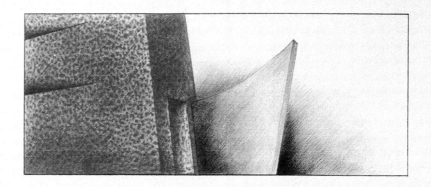

2   Rendering of entry details.
3   Photomontage with rendering of the front elevation.

4   View of the street-side facade.

5   Detail view.

6   Model.

7   Lobby entrance from the street, showing
    cemetery beyond. Photo: Nacasa & Partners.

8 Lobby interior with entry stair.
   Photo: Nacasa and Partners.
9 Typical office interior.

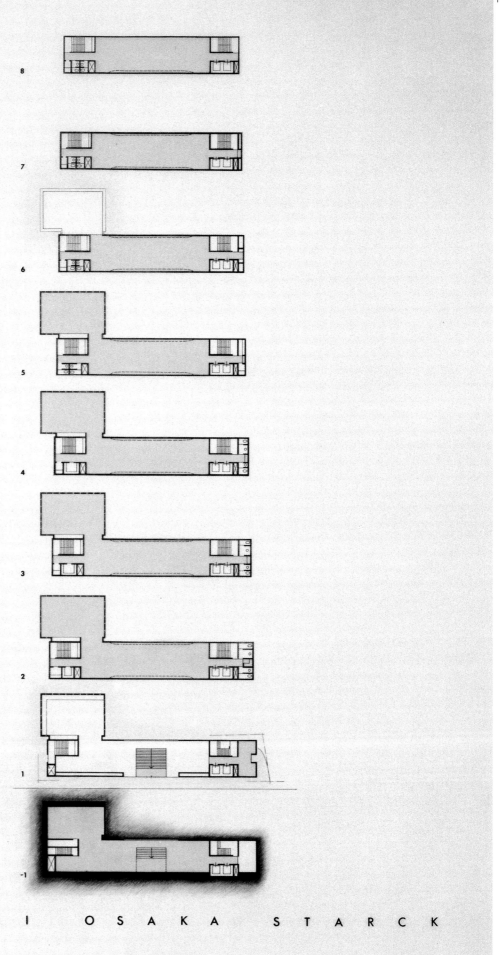

M E I S E I   O S A K A   S T A R C K

10 Floor-plan series.
11 Sketch of the elevator core.
12 Sketch of an interior detail.
13 Lobby-level plan.

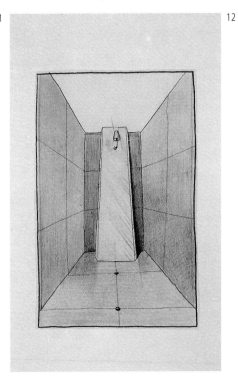

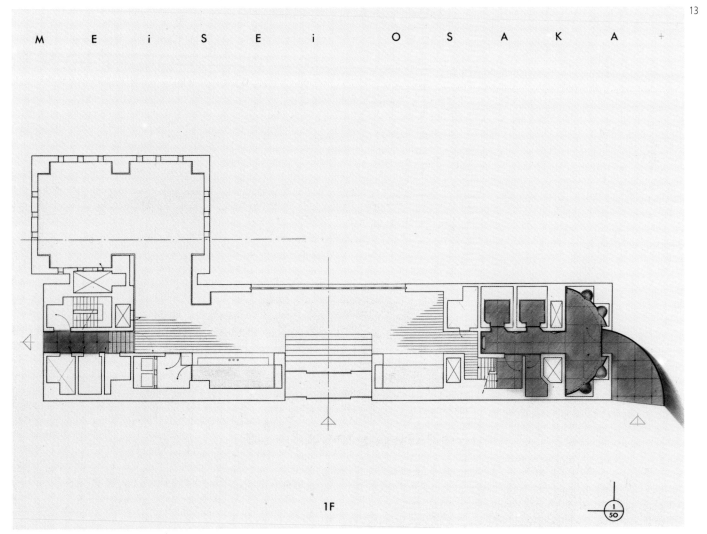

M E i S E i O S A K A +

1F

MEISEI OSAKA STARCK

14 Front elevation.
15 Longitudinal section.
16 Transversal section.

M E I S E I   O S A K A   S T A R C K

M E I S E I   O S A K A   S T A R C K

SIMON UNGERS AND TOM KINSLOW

Simon Ungers, Architect

T-House

Wilton, New York
Completed: 1992

When commissioning Simon Ungers to build his residence on a 40-acre site in upstate New York, writer Lawrence Marcelle prescribed a clear separation of living and working spaces. In response, the architect obliged by dividing the programs of residence and library into two rectangular blocks and stacking those blocks perpendicularly atop one another. The entry hall between acts as a transitional space, connecting the library above to the living quarters below. Partially submerged into the southward-sloping site, the residence subordinates itself to the 10,000-volume library, which cantilevers 14 feet out from either side of the floors below, the orientation from which the building derives its name.

Prior to construction, Kinslow joined in partnership with Ungers to collaborate on the development and realization of the project. Situated at the edge of an abandoned sand quarry, the T-House overlooks the Berkshire Mountains from its position between a cleared field to the east and dense woods to the west. The lower floor contains the residential spaces within a single, linear volume oriented east–west and differentiated by core elements. The kitchen, steel chimney, and bathroom serve to define and separate spaces for dining, living, and sleeping within the residence's 84-foot length. Hardwood floors throughout complement wall panels of plywood veneer. In contrast, the bathroom and kitchen fixtures are stainless steel components that the architects selected from prison and commercial suppliers.

In designing the 44-foot-long and 16-foot-wide library, Ungers and Kinslow considered both the distant mountain views and the protection of books. Within the double-story room, their solution provides a windowless mezzanine comprised of an independent steel structure hung from the ceiling and suspended above a reading space with windows. A dumbwaiter enables easy transportation of books between floors. Below, in the reading space, eight-foot-high openings puncture the exterior surface at two-foot intervals. Swinging wooden panels inside the space allow for controlled light and views.

Throughout the exterior and interior surfaces of the 2,500-square-foot residence, Ungers and Kinslow employed a similar proportioning system consisting of two-foot-wide by eight-foot-high panels and openings. The construction, hull-like in its distinction between inner and outer layers, provides the impression of a seamless structure from the outside. Creating this effect required seam-welding quarter-inch weathering plates to a steel channel frame. The shell was prefabricated in six components, each of which was then delivered to the site on flatbed trucks and assembled by crane on top of a concrete foundation. The resultant oxidized surface gives a continuous and homogeneous effect, due to the welding and sanding procedures and the absence of expansion joints.

Interior joints, however, are revealed. The architects specified three-quarter-inch plywood veneer panels assembled in a tongue-and-groove method and divided by quarter-inch seams to expose the construction method. The different expansion rates of wood and steel necessitated that this wooden structure be independent of the external steel frame. Windows throughout are fashioned from black enamel steel. In addition, Ungers and Kinslow used steel grating for the library's shelving systems, mezzanine structure, and stairs in order to increase the internal impression of transparency within the strict volume defined by the seamless exterior skin.

1   Rear elevation.
    Photo: Eduard Hueber.

2   Winter view from the woods.
     Photo: Eduard Hueber.
3   Entry elevation.
     Photo: Eduard Hueber.

2

5

6

4   Library interior.
     Photo: Eduard Hueber.
5   Living room interior.
     Photo: Eduard Hueber.
6   Bathroom interior.
     Photo: Eduard Hueber.

7   Factory view of the library under construction.
     Photo: Eduard Hueber.

8   Library unit being transported on a flatbed
     truck to the site.
     Photo: Eduard Hueber.

9   Library being assembled by crane.
     Photo: Eduard Hueber.

10   Presentation model.
      Photo: Eduard Hueber.

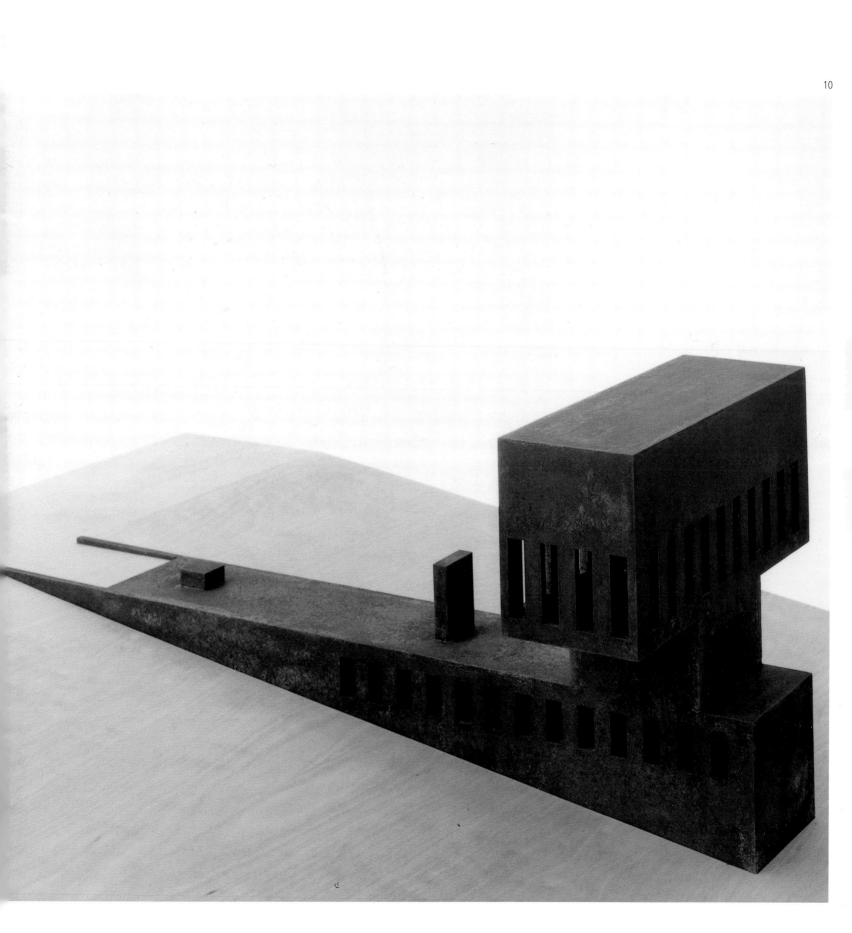

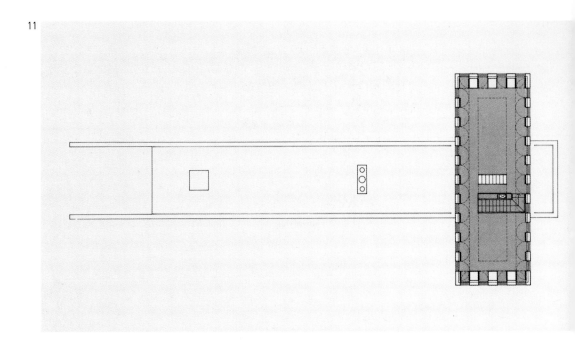

11

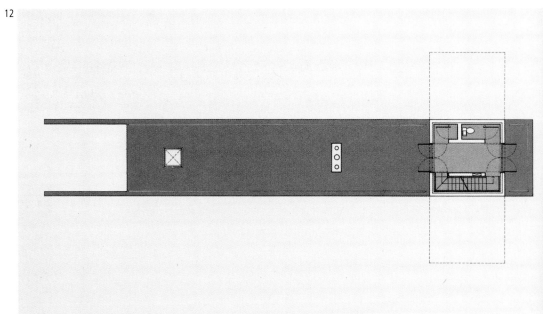

12

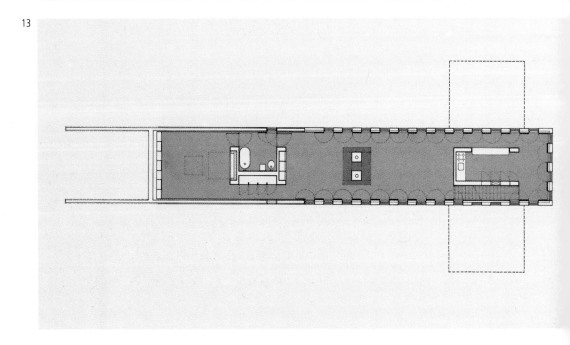

13

11 Library-level plan.
12 Entry-level plan.
13 Main-level plan.
14 Back elevation and transversal section.
15 Side elevation.
16 Longitudinal section.
17 Longitudinal section.

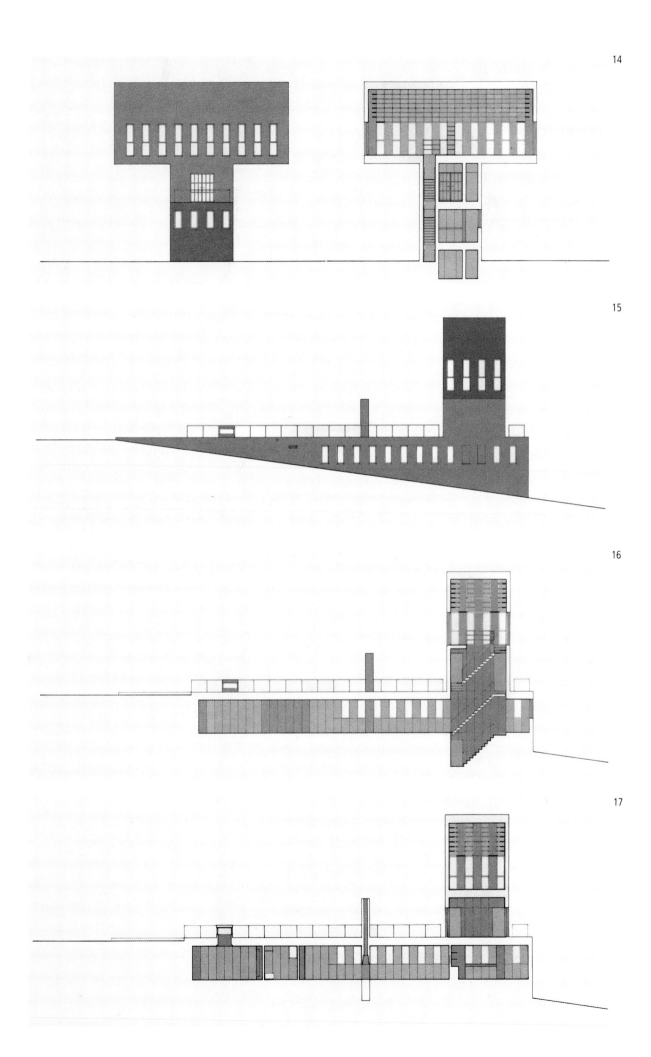

PETER EISENMAN

Eisenman Architects is a 30-person firm with an international reputation for producing bold and critically acclaimed architecture. Born in 1932, principal Peter Eisenman, FAIA, is known as a theorist, architect, and educator. He received a bachelor of architecture degree from Cornell University, a master of architecture degree from Columbia University, and M.A. and Ph.D. degrees from Cambridge University. In 1980, after many years of teaching and writing, Mr. Eisenman established his professional practice to focus exclusively on building. He has designed a wide range of prototypical projects, including large-scale housing and urban design schemes, educational facilities, and a series of private houses. In 1985, Mr. Eisenman received first prize at the third international architectural Biennale in Venice, and his project for social housing in Berlin was featured on a postage stamp commemorating the 750th anniversary of that city. He founded and directed the Institute for Architecture and Urban Studies, a think-tank for architectural criticism, and has received numerous awards, including a Guggenheim Fellowship. Mr Eisenman's academic involvement has included teaching at Cambridge University and at Harvard, Yale, and Princeton universities. He is the author of several articles, essays, and books, and his projects have been exhibited around the world.

REM KOOLHAAS

Rem Koolhaas, founder/principal of Office for Metropolitan Architecture (OMA), was born in Rotterdam in 1944. As well as participating in numerous competitions and exhibitions internationally, Mr. Koolhaas is the author of the influential book Delirious New York: A Retroactive Manifesto for Manhattan (1978) and the more recent OMA: S M L XL (1995). He has held teaching positions in London and Delft, as well as in the United States at Harvard University and the University of California, Los Angeles. Built projects and works in progress include both public and private structures and urban development schemes. A recipient of the Progressive Architecture Award and the Antonio Gaudí Prize, Mr. Koolhaas was named a visiting scholar at the Getty Center for The History of Art and the Humanities in 1993.

PHILIPPE SAMYN

Philippe Samyn, senior managing partner of Samyn and Partners, became a founding partner of the firm after two years of training with a firm of consulting engineers and six years with the architectural office of A. De Doncker. He is responsible for the design of every project commissioned to Samyn Partners. Born in 1948, Mr. Samyn studied engineering, urban planning and management, and architecture in Belgium and the United States. In addition to participating in various international exhibitions since 1989, he has lectured at academic institutions in Belgium.

RAFAEL MONEO

José Rafael Moneo was born in Spain in 1937. He obtained his architecture degree in 1961 from the Madrid University School of Architecture. In 1970, he was named chaired professor in architectural theory at the Esquela Técnica Superior de Arquitectura de Barcelona and in 1980, chaired professor at the Esquela Técnica Superior de Arquitectura de Madrid, where he taught until 1985. During the late '70s and early '80s, Mr. Moneo was a visiting professor at Princeton and Harvard universities, as well as at the Ecole Polytechnique Fédérale in Lausanne, Switzerland. In 1985, he was named chairman of the Architecture Department of the Harvard University Graduate School of Design, a position he held until the end of 1990. He was granted the honorary Sert Professorship at Harvard in 1992. In the same year, Mr. Moneo was awarded the Medalla de Oro de Bellas Artes by the Spanish government. He is a member of the American Academy of Arts and Letters and honorary fellow of the American Institute of Architects.

JEAN NOUVEL

The French architect and urban planner Jean Nouvel was born in 1945. In 1972, he received his architecture degree in Paris. In the early 1980s, Mr. Nouvel founded and directed the Biennale d'Architecture, part of the Biennale de Paris. He has been named Chevalier dans l'Ordre des Arts et des Lettres, and has been the recipient of numerous awards, including the Grand Prix d'Architecture and an Architectural Record award. Since 1991, he has been vice president of the Institut Français d'Architecture. In 1993, he was made honorary fellow of the American Institute of Architects (Chicago).

PHILIPPE STARCK

Born in France in 1949, Philippe Starck loved drawing as a child. He remembers his father's work as an aeronautical engineer as especially inspirational. In 1968, embarking on a career during which he would transform many objects of daily life — from lemon squeezers to light fixtures, ashtrays to armchairs — into witty, whimsical, but nonetheless utilitarian visions, Mr. Starck set up his first company. Having achieved a certain notoriety as an interior designer, he went on to create or help create individual and innovative structures and spaces, often on a massive scale. He has remodeled hotels in New York, created office buildings in Japan, designed houses and apartment blocks in Europe and the United States, and participated in exhibitions all over the world. Mr. Starck has been the recipient of numerous prizes and awards, including the Grand Prix du Design Industriel and the Oscar du Design, and has been named Créateur de l'Année in France.

JACQUES HERZOG AND PIERRE DE MEURON

The founders of Herzog & de Meuron were both born in 1950. All of the partners of the firm were born in Switzerland and received architecture degrees from the ETH in Zurich. Jacques Herzog and Pierre de Meuron went into partnership in 1978; Harry Gugger and Christine Binswanger became partners in 1991 and 1994, respectively. In addition to their work as practicing architects, both Mr. Herzog and Mr. de Meuron have been visiting professors at Harvard University. The firm's international exposure began in 1989 with exhibitions in Europe and, later, the United States. Among Herzog & de Meuron's awards has been the Kunstpreis der Akademie der Kunste, Berlin. Monographs about their work have appeared in several languages.

FARSHID MOUSSAVI AND ALEJANDRO ZAERA-POLO

The London firm of Foreign Office Architects was co-founded by Farshid Moussavi and Alejandro Zaera-Polo. Ms. Moussavi, who was born in Iran in 1965 and studied architecture in England and the United States, is a unit master at the AA, London, and a design critic at the Sint Lucas Architectuur Instituut in Ghent. She has been a member of OMA in Rotterdam, as well as of the Renzo Piano Building Workshop in Genoa. Born in Spain in 1963, Mr. Zaera-Polo, who studied there and in the United States, is also a unit master at the AA, London. He was a design critic at the Escuela Técnica Superior de Arquitectura de Madrid and, like Ms. Moussavi, a member of OMA. He has published frequently in Croquis as well as in various other periodicals, including Quaderns, AD, Arch+, and de Architect.

SIMON UNGERS AND TOM KINSLOW

Both Simon Ungers and Tom Kinslow were born in 1957, Ungers in Germany, Kinslow in New York State. In 1969, Mr. Ungers emigrated to the United States, and in 1980 he received a bachelor of architecture degree from Cornell University. Following graduation, he founded the firm of UKZ (Ungers-Kiss-Zwigard) in Ithaca, New York. After teaching and practicing in upstate New York, Mr. Ungers moved to New York City in 1986, setting up a practice there. He has since worked extensively in the United States and Europe, participating in a number of international competitions and exhibitions, and his realized projects include three houses and an addition to a vineyard. He has been the recipient of two citations from Progressive Architecture magazine and recently won a first prize for the Holocaust Memorial Competition in Berlin. Mr. Kinslow worked for UKZ in Ithaca before graduating from Syracuse University in 1988. He later worked on the T-House and set up his own practice in 1992.

Project Credits

The Max Reinhardt Haus
Berlin, Germany

Clients: Advanta Management AG Dieter Bock
OSTINVEST Klaus-Peter Junge Dieter Klaus
Architect: Eisenman Architects, PC
Principal-in-Charge: Peter Eisenman, FAIA
Associate-in-Charge: George Kewin, AIA
Project Architects: Richard Labonte; Edward Mitchell;
Lindy Roy
Project Team: Armand Biglari, Brad Gildea, Norbert
Holthausen, Gregory Luhan, Stefania Rinaldi, David
Schatzle, Jon Stephens
Project Assistants: Federico Beulcke, Mark Bretler,
Andrew Burmeister, Robert Holten, Patrick Keane, Brad
Khouri, Joseph Lau, Vincent LeFeuvre, Fabian Lemmel,
John Maze, Steven Meyer, Debbie Park, Silke Potting,
Benjamin Wade
Consultants:
Landscape Architect: Hanna/Olin, Ltd., Laurie Olin,
Shirley Kressel, Matthew W. White
Color Consultant: Donald Kaufman Color
Structural Engineer: Severud Associates Edward M.
Messina, Edward DiPaolo
Mechanical Engineer: Jaros, Baum & Bolles, Augustine
A. DiGiacomo, Kenneth J. Zuar
Wind and Shadow: Spacetec Studies Datengewinnung
Cost Estimating: Donnell Consultants, Inc. Steward
Donnell
Computer Images: Edward Keller
Photography: Dick Frank Studios

Signal Box auf dem Wolf
Basel, Switzerland

Client/Owner: SBB Kreis 2, Swiss Federal Railway
Architect: Herzog and de Meuron
Project Management: Proplan Ing. AG
HVAC Engineer: SEC-AG
Electrical Engineer: Selmoni AG
Facade: Tecton AG
Models: H. & de M./Hermann Fürlinger

Sea Terminal
Zeebrugge, Belgium

Client: Port Authority Zeebrugge
Principal Architect: OMA/Rem Koolhaas
Engineers: Ove Arup & Partners, London
Model: Parthesius & de Rijk, Werkplaats, Rotterdam

Kursaal Cultural Center and Auditorium
San Sebastián, Spain

Client: Municipality of San Sebastián-Donostia
Architect: Rafael Moneo
Architect-in-charge: Luis Rojo
Project Architects: Eduardo Belzunce, Collette Creppell,
Luis Díaz Mauriño, Fernando Iznaola, Ignacio Quemada,
Robert Robinowitz, Adolfo Zanetti
Structural Engineer: Javier Manterola
Technical Consulting: J.G. Asociados
Acoustical Consultant: Higini Arau
Models: Juan de Dios and Jesús del Rey

Yokohama International Port Terminal
Yokohama, Japan

Client: Yokohama Port Authority, City of Yokohama
Architect: Foreign Office Architects (Farshid Moussavi
and Alejandro Zaera-Polo)
Collaborators: Yoon King Chong, Michael Cosmas,
Jung-Hyun Hwang, Kazugo Ninomiya
Engineering Advisers: Ove Arup & Partners
Models: Andrew Ingham Associates
Media: Ivan Ascanio, Guy Westbrook

The New National Theater
Tokyo, Japan

Client: The Ministry of Buildings
Architect: Jean Nouvel and Associates (Emmanuel
Blamont, Jean-Marc Ibos, Myrto Vitart)
Designer: Philippe Starck
Scenographer: Jacques Le Marquet

Collaborators: Marie-France Baldran, Bruno Borrione,
Mathilde Brasilier, Christian Chenus, François
Fauconnet, Tristan Fourtine, Christian Gavoille, Vincent
Lafont, Damien Lécuyer, Frédérique Valette
Computer Images: Presles-Design
Perspective Renderings: François Seigneur, Fabrice Viney
Office of Scenographic Studies: Michel Seban
Engineer: Technip
Model: Etienne Follenfant

Walloon Forestry Department Shell
Marche-en-Famenne, Belgium

Client: Belgian Ministry of the Environment
Architects and Engineers: Samyn and Partners (Philippe
Samyn, Ghislain André, Jean Luc Capron, André
Charon, Christine Fontaine, Serge Peeters, Dalip Singh)
Stability: Philippe Samyn, Guy Clantin
Services: Philippe Samyn, Paul Fontaine, A. De Windt
(thermodynamic calculation)
Model: Marie Moignot, Quentin Cruysmans

The Baron Vert
Osaka, Japan

Client: Meisei Engineering Company Ltd.
Architect: Philippe Starck
Project Management: Meisei Engineering Company Ltd.
Contractor: Ohayashi Gumi
Photography: Hiroyuki Hirai

T-House
Wilton, New York

Client: Lawrence Marcelle
Architects: Simon Ungers and Tom Kinslow with Matt
Altwicker, Tom Ogorzaleck, Mary Langan
Engineers: Ryan and Biggs Assoc.
Contractors: STS Inc. (steel shell) Regenerative Building
Construction
Photography: Arch Photo—-Eduard Hueber
Model: The Model Shop at Products for Research, Inc.
(Robert Martin, Director)